CHILD SEXUAL ABUSERS

Child Sexual Abusers
A Community Treatment Approach

Jackie Craissati
Oxleas NHS Trust, Bexley, UK

Psychology Press Ltd, Publishers
27 Church Road
Hove
East Sussex, BN3 2FA
UK

British Library Cataloguing-in-Publication Data

A catalogue record for this book is available from the British Library

ISBN 0-86377-734-1

Typeset by Graphicraft Limited, Hong Kong
Printed and bound in the UK by Biddles Ltd, Guildford and King's Lynn

Contents

Acknowledgements

Much of the material for this book has arisen as a result of my involvement in the Challenge Project, and I am indebted to the psychologists at the Bracton Centre and the Inner London Probation Service officers who have worked as group and individual therapists, supervisors and managers; in particular I would like to thank Grace McClurg for her invaluable contribution to the research and evaluation components of the Project.

I am grateful for the advice offered by Anna Motz and Nigel Warburton during the preliminary stages of preparing the book, and have valued comments made by Grace and Anna on my first draft. The Bracton Centre and the Psychology Department, both of Oxleas NHS Trust, have been most supportive in allowing me time to write, the Trust library has provided me with a steady flow of publications, and I have appreciated the warm response of colleagues to the project.

CHAPTER ONE

Introduction

... "By this time I was in a state of excitement bordering on insanity; but I also had the cunning of the insane. Sitting there, on the sofa, I managed to attune, by a series of stealthy movements, my masked lust to her guileless limbs. It was no easy matter to divert the little maiden's attention while I performed the obscure adjustments necessary for the success of the trick. Talking fast, lagging behind my own breath, catching up with it, mimicking a sudden toothache to explain the breaks in my patter—and all the while keeping a maniac's inner eye on my distant golden goal, I cautiously increased the magic friction that was doing away, in an illusional, if not factual, sense, with the physically irremovable, but psychologically very friable texture of the material divide (pajamas and robe) between the weight of two sunburnt legs, resting athwart my lap, and the hidden tumor of an unspeakable passion . . ." (from *Lolita*, Nabokov, 1955).

It may appear frivolous to begin a discussion of perpetrators of child sexual abuse with a quote from Lolita, and yet little has been written which so eloquently describes the mind of a man sexually fixated on a pubescent girl: his infatuation with what she represents rather than who she is; his distorted interpretation of her responses to him; his focused, persistent and ruthless cunning in achieving his desired goal; and the erotic lyricism which almost—but not entirely—masks his sordid lust. Unfortunately, few child sexual offenders are able to articulate their thoughts and feelings with such insight, and the behavioural focus of the victim interviews for legal purposes (searching to establish whether fondling, masturbation or penetration took place) only reduces the offences to a series of sexual acts. Those practitioners who are involved in the assessment and management of perpetrators of child sexual abuse have to set feelings of abhorrence and mystification to one side in order to try to understand the motivations and internal

1

worlds of such offenders, so as to try and develop a strategy to reduce the risk of further offending.

CURRENT CONCERNS

In setting the scene for a discussion of perpetrators of child sexual abuse, this chapter aims to place these offenders within the current context in Britain. Sex offenders form a very high profile group of offenders; they provoke strong feelings in the general public and pose a considerable challenge to the professionals who are involved in their assessment and management. In recent years, there has been a burgeoning of treatment programmes targeting sex offenders—an emphasis which has not been matched with other groups of offenders (Barker & Beech, 1993). Furthermore, the Criminal Justice Act (1991) specifically addressed the issue with the following points:

1. Sex offenders can now be required to attend a probation programme or to take part in required activities for the full duration of the probation order.
2. When considering offences of a violent or sexual nature, a longer sentence than might otherwise be justified by the seriousness of the offence can be passed, when this is necessary to protect the public from serious harm by the offender.
3. Sex offenders sentenced to 12 months or more can be required to be supervised up to the end of their sentence (rather than the 3/4 point).

As this book was being written, the requirement for convicted sex offenders in the community to register with their local police was established (Sex Offenders Act, 1997): this attempt to monitor the whereabouts of perpetrators offers reassurance—perhaps falsely—to the public and but certainly might lay the foundation for a coordinated and responsive multi-agency approach to the management of some high risk offenders. Further proposals are under discussion and may soon become legislation: that sex offenders can be banned from entering public places which places the community at risk (such as parks or swimming pools); and that courts should have the power to require an extended supervision period in the community following release from a determinate sentence imposed for a sexual offence.

Media interest has reflected—and perhaps fuelled—public concern, particularly with regard to child sexual abuse. Following the implementation of registration, a national Sunday paper published an article titled "In Your Back Yard. The man on the left (silhouetted profile); is a known paedophile. Despite a new register of sex offenders, you are still not allowed to know if somebody like him is living in your area, watching your child. But if you did, it might make him even more dangerous" (Sunday Times). As never before, professionals in the field are under scrutiny, criticised at times for the emphasis on treatment rather than punishment, at other times for failing to engage high risk offenders in treatment. At a time when the public and the government are predominantly emphasising external controls, the question should be raised as to whether a treatment approach—relying as it does on self-controls—is justified at all. There is a growing body of evidence, laid out in this book, to suggest that not all perpetrators reoffend, and some not for long periods of time; that some treatment programmes for some perpetrators have reduced reoffending rates; and that treatment, alongside other child protection measures, has allowed some fathers and children to re-establish a warm and close relationship. Furthermore, there are concerns that excessive emphasis on external and potentially punitive controls may in fact increase an offender's social and emotional instability, paradoxically raising the risk of reoffending. However practitioners, in apparently embracing the principles of a treatment approach to sex offenders alongside other measures, must be prepared to justify the approach with a clear and objective rationale for assessment, treatment and evaluation.

THE EXTENT OF THE PROBLEM: ASSUMPTIONS AND MYTHS

The current state of knowledge on sex offenders is problematic, predominantly for two reasons: methodological and mythological reasons. In the former case, attempts to evaluate recidivism and treatment outcome have been dogged by inertia, poor sampling techniques, geographical bias and a lack of effective comparative data (see Chapter seven for a detailed outline of the difficulties). The result is that few generalisations can be made from the available data, particularly as much of it originates from America and Canada; in this country, until recently, the sparse research has been institutionally (often prison) based.

Clinical definitions of sexual abuse of children have tended to utilise three dimensions: an age difference of five years or more between child and offender; specific sexual behaviours, such as kissing, fondling genitalia, oral sex, penetration of the vagina/anus with objects or penis, exhibitionism and photography; and sexual intent, an area which can be difficult to determine. There is little consistent agreement on the way in which familial and cultural norms can influence the decision to define behaviour as abuse.

Criminal statistics show that in 1995 in England and Wales, 4600 men and 100 women were sentenced by the courts for indictable sexual offences and a further 2250 were cautioned (Home Office, 1995). When the figures are broken down further to those offenders where the victim was known to be aged under 16, there were 1350 cautions, 3284 prosecutions and 2554 convictions (of which 34, 30 and 19 respectively were female offenders). The criminal justice response to child sexual abusers is highlighted by the following data for the most common offence types in 1995 (Home Office, 1995):

1. *Indecent assault on a female aged <16* resulted in 1440 convictions (1787 prosecutions); 31% received a community sentence and 57% immediate custody.
2. *Indecent assault on a male aged <16* resulted in 331 convictions (392 prosecutions); 29% received a community sentence and 61% immediate custody.
3. *Unlawful sexual intercourse with a girl aged <16* resulted in 203 convictions (195 prosecutions); 33% received a community sentence and 42% immediate custody.
4. *Rape of a female aged <16* resulted in 111 convictions (330 prosecutions); 4% received a community sentence and 84% immediate custody.

Between 1990 and 1994, an average of 22% of victims of rape were aged between 10 and 15 and a further 4% were aged less than nine; the risk of attacks by strangers remained very low. In terms of indecent assaults, overall female victims tended to be older than male victims: approximately half of female victims were aged under 16 (and 17% aged less than 10) whilst over two-thirds of male victims were aged under 16 (27% being aged less than 10). One in five of victims aged between 0 and 9 were assaulted by someone aged between 10 and 15.

There is little doubt that under-reporting is problematic with regard to sexual offenders. The British Crime Survey (Home Office, 1988) estimated the report rate for rape and indecent assault as 17%, similar to rates for other crimes against the person, and whilst official Home Office statistics for 1989 showed that reported sex offences increased by 40% between 1979 and 1989, they still only accounted for less than 1% of recorded crime. More recent figures in the Home Office statistics (Home Office, 1995), state that there were 30,000 notifiable sexual offences recorded by the police, up 4% on previous years in line with other offences, and they suggest that the British Crime Survey, 1995, indicates that there is a fourfold underestimate for most offences. The law in relation to child sexual abuse offers very little in the way of a true picture: offenders may only be convicted of "specimen" charges when abuse has occurred over a lengthy period or with a number of victims; charges are likely to be dropped, particularly when victims are young, or reduced to a lesser charge in order to avoid a trial. A recent study of convicted perpetrators of child sexual abuse in southeast London (Craissati, 1994) showed that charges were more than twice as likely to be dropped when victims were under the age of ten, and that 47% of initial rape and buggery charges were dropped/reduced to indecent assault before trial. Clearly indecent assault encompasses behaviour ranging from touching the genital area outside clothing to profoundly invasive acts such as oral sex and penetration with objects.

Social services child protection teams manage families where children have been identified as being at serious risk of sexual abuse, although the majority of alleged perpetrators have not been prosecuted. Craissati and McClurg (internal document, 1995) found that between 0 and 8% of these alleged perpetrators in two London boroughs were convicted as a result of the allegations. British estimates of the prevalence of sexual abuse in the general population, based on randomised retrospective studies of adults (Baker & Duncan, 1985) reported that 12% of females and 8% of males had been sexually abused before the age of 16.

Attempts to explore the potential offending rate in the general population have alarmed practitioners who tend to quote the finding that about one-fifth of college males reported having some sexual attraction to children (Briere & Runtz, 1989). Yet there is little to substantiate the validity of these self-report studies in terms of sexual interests and, more importantly, propensity to act out those interests, particularly against prepubertal children. We know that many 'normal' people have deviant sexual fantasies and that deviant sexual arousal profiles can be obtained from non-sexual offenders under certain conditions (Quinsey, Chaplin, & Varney, 1981). Nevertheless, it is probable—but as yet unproven—that there is a considerable barrier between fantasy and action in the general population.

In terms of mythology, practitioner attitudes towards sex offenders are usually derived from a handful of research findings which have led to illogical and inaccurate rhetoric. Some of these falacious assertions are discussed by Mair (1996) and outlined below. For example, Abel, Becker, Mittetman, Cunningham-Rathner, Rouleau, and Murphy (1987) wrote an extraordinarily frequently cited paper regarding the multiple sexually deviant activities of non incarcerated sex offenders who were offered treatment in return for confidential confessions regarding their sexual misbehaviour to date. Clearly such offenders who voluntarily seek treatment outside a prosecution are both highly unusual, and likely to represent the most disturbed and deviant of the population; furthermore the average offending rate is often quoted as being in the 100s, whilst few pause to note that the majority of individuals in the study offended against a few victims on a few occasions, the minority accounting for the distortion in the mean because of their prolific sexual activity. Clearly this highlights a need to be cautious in interpreting studies that extrapolate estimates of the number of abusers from prevalence studies of adult survivors of abuse, or that rely on accumulated individual acts of abuse (an incest abuser can account for 36 'paraphilic' acts by indecently assaulting his daughter once a month over a three year period).

Retrospective studies are particularly prone to distortion because of sampling problems: for example, many serious adult sexual offenders are known as having commenced their deviant sexual interests and activities in adolescence, yet few researchers have attempted to establish a baseline rate for sexually aggressive behaviour in adolescence—although Scully (1990) found that minor sexual offences were admitted to just as frequently by prisoners who had never been convicted of a sexual offence as by convicted rapists. We know that men with previous sexual convictions are more likely to get further sexual convictions, but there is a tendency to assume that undiscovered sexual offending has the same predictive power; this assumption must be based on the premise that conviction and punishment has no impact on any man in terms of his sexual habits or his motivation and capacity to refrain from further offending.

Emotive responses to biased assumptions can only increase the daunting task of assessing and managing the sexual offenders known within our system, and identifying those individuals who do indeed pose an enormous risk to children. The message that "there is no cure" is both disheartening and probably untrue: it would seem that—despite under-reporting—a number of convicted sex offenders do not sexually reoffend. If, therefore, some of them have abstained from acting out their impulses or desires, it raises the question why they are treated differently from any abstaining offender (or indeed client presenting with disturbed mental health symptoms) who inevitably carries with them a risk—under certain circumstances—of reverting to former behaviour.

TREATMENT RESOURCES IN BRITAIN

There are innumerable community-based treatment programmes, mostly on a small scale, and managed by probation, sometimes in cooperation with forensic mental health services. The only residential service exclusively targeting sex offenders is run by the Faithful Foundation in southeast England, a charitable organisation which offers an intensive treatment programme to men funded mainly by social services and probation. Within the prison system, the Sex Offender Treatment Programme (SOTP) was launched in 1991, and aims to assess and treat all sex offenders (prepared to cooperate) serving a sentence of four or more years. Thornton and Hogue (1993) reported that by 1994, over 700 incarcerated sex offenders will have been treated on the SOTP, an enormous improvement on the previously patchy service available, although still falling far short of the 3283 male sex offenders within the prison system in 1992. More recent estimates from David Thornton (personal correspondence, 1998) indicate that approximately 1400 males are sentenced to at least two years imprisonment for a sexual offence each year, and it is expected that 600 sex offenders complete the SOTP each year, the vast majority of whom are child sexual abusers. Far fewer sex offenders are managed by the National Health Service: clearly severely mentally ill sex offenders can be sectioned under the Mental Health Act (1983) and potentially treated in medium and high security hospitals. However, the use of the category of Psychopathic Disorder in the Mental Health Act (1983) in relation to personality disordered offenders, is rather more controversial, and it is probably true to say that greater attention is paid these days to the treatability criteria, resulting in a more cautious approach to hospital transfer.

Nearly all the treatment approaches to the non-mentally ill sex offenders are currently based on a cognitive–behavioural model of psychological functioning, much of which is derived from American and Canadian practitioners. The only specialist centre for the provision of psychoanalytic psychotherapy to offenders is the Portman Clinic in northwest London. Whilst the probation service has been at the forefront of running treatment projects, Barker and Beech (1993) pointed out that of the 63 programmes run by 43 probation services, only 3 had been running for more than five years, and that there has been a dearth of evaluative work in the area. In southeast London over the past five years, the author has been part of a multi-agency project to provide a comprehensive assessment and treatment programme to perpetrators of child sexual abuse living (or returning) to the community: the Challenge Project has many features in common with the majority of treatment programmes in Britain, although senior management commitment from the various agencies involved has ensured that it could evolve without undue reliance on the enthusiasm of one or two committed practitioner/therapists. Unusually, the treatment programme has been carefully evaluated, including follow-up of both treated and untreated child sexual abusers, and this research is detailed in Chapter seven (Craissati & McClurg, 1996, 1997). As the Project is fairly representative of the work currently being pursued, it will be repeatedly referred to throughout the book.

THE AIM OF THE BOOK

The aim of this book is to provide a practice-based model for informing the assessment, treatment and evaluation of perpetrators of child sexual abuse in the community. However it must be stated at the outset that no text can provide a substitute for training, supervision, experience, and expert consultation. The current state of knowledge regarding the assessment and treatment of perpetrators of child sexual abuse is a complex and, at times, uncertain affair: it is the responsibility of all practitioners and their managers to ensure that they work with the scope of their professional expertise. It has been a deliberate strategy to avoid presenting the reader with comprehensive research data and references, particularly those pertaining to studies outside Britain; rather key texts have been highlighted which should be referred to in cases of special interest.

The emphasis on a cognitive–behavioural model of treatment is not intended to imply that this is the only effective means of intervention for all child abusers: rather it has been chosen because it relates most closely to the knowledge base of many British practitioners such as probation officers and psychologists; its offence-focused approach falls in line with the expectations of the courts; it provides a means of intervening with perpetrators whose motivation for treatment is ambivalent at best; and there is some evidence (see Chapter seven) to suggest that it may provide the optimum means of reducing the risk of re-offending. For these reasons, the cognitive–behavioural approach, as adopted by the Challenge Project and many other treatment programmes, will be outlined in step-by-step detail. However, there is nothing intrinsically unique about the Challenge Project programme, derived as it is from a variety of sources, and practitioners may wish to omit or add to the programme according to their own experience and perceived needs of their group of offenders.

The emphasis on adult child sexual abusers in the book allows for a more complete consideration of this group of offenders, their responses to treatment, and the problems they may pose. However, it is anticipated that much of the assessment and treatment material will be relevant to sexual offenders against adults, adolescent, and female sex offenders. Although much of the information can be generalised to female sex offenders, they are not directly commented on in the book: there is no doubt that it is the men who pose the greatest burden on resources and the greatest risk to the public. For example in 1992 there were 11 female in relation to over 3000 male sex offenders within the prison system, and it is for this reason that this book—and the majority of treatment programmes— target men. For simplicity, the sexual offenders will be referred to as "he" and "perpetrator" will be used to denote sexual offenders against children.

Both assessment and treatment considerations, without reference to the clients themselves, loses much of their relevance, and considerable emphasis will be placed in the ensuing chapters on clinical vignettes to illustrate both the principles and problems of practice. Four men have been drawn from the Challenge Project—Tom, Peter, George, and Kevin—whose details have been altered to ensure confidentiality, but who are representative of the larger sample of clients. Their progress—successful or otherwise—through the assessment, treatment and follow up phases of the Project will be detailed.

> **Tom** was referred at the point of parole. He had been convicted of three counts of indecent assault on his daughter, Mary, over a five year period when she was aged 8–13. He received a six year sentence, and was granted parole with a condition to attend the Challenge Project.
>
> **Peter**, aged 48, was referred at the sentencing stage. He was convicted of one charge of indecent assault on a five-year-old girl who lived down his road. He had previous convictions for rape and buggery on pre-pubescent girls. Given the relatively minor nature of his index offence, he was given a probation order with a condition to attend the Challenge Project.
>
> **George**, aged 22, was referred informally, having completed a five year sentence for the indecent assault of his step-nephew John, between the ages of 7–12. He subsequently married and asked for treatment because of his fear of re-offending.
>
> **Kevin**, aged 35, was referred at the sentencing stage. He was charged with the indecent assault of his 12-year-old step-daughter, Sally, over a four month period. He received a probation order with a condition to attend the Challenge Project.

Chapter two provides an overview of the main theoretical perspectives— multi-factorial, psychodynamic, and cognitive–behavioural—before considering the complexities of assessment and risk prediction in chapter three. Chapter four is devoted to managing denial, perhaps the most difficult area for practitioners who may be overwhelmed by and enraged with the entrenched resistance and grossly distorted thinking of many perpetrators. The parameters of treatment are considered in Chapter five, including consideration of suitability for different modes of treatment, issues of confidentiality and the implications of statutory requirements. Chapter six outlines the suggested treatment model in detail, and addresses some of the difficulties in the process as well as the content of treatment. Finally, in Chapter seven, the problems of evaluation will be critically considered, including a review of key recent British studies evaluating treatment efficacy.

CHAPTER TWO

Theoretical principles

Theoretical principles underpinning the sexual abuse of children can be all too easily forgotten in the current climate: the expectation that all convicted—and where possible, unconvicted—perpetrators should be treated either in the prison system or in the community poses a tremendous burden upon those professionals involved in their care and supervision. The uncritical enthusiasm for a single model of intervention—currently the cognitive–behavioural approach, but formerly both psychodynamic and family systems models were popular—may lead to overoptimistic expectations, outright failures, therapeutic hopelessness and an inefficient use of scarce resources.

A basic working knowledge of the main theoretical approaches will always inform practice, and provides an important intellectual defence against the emotionally draining nature of the offences, and the resistance to change which is so often encountered in these perpetrators. Furthermore both theoretically-based and empirically-based frameworks can offer a valid basis for evaluating future risk, treatability, and change in the perpetrator.

For the sake of clarity, the wide range of theoretical perspectives have been subsumed into three main categories: multi-factorial frameworks; psychodynamic; and cognitive–behavioural approaches. These are not mutually exclusive categories and often it will appear that apparently disparate theories are describing similar processes in different language. It is advisable to read the original texts for a full understanding of any of the theoretical approaches, but for the purposes of this summary, some understanding of the relevant terminology is assumed.

MULTI-FACTORIAL MODELS

Multi-factorial models may be empirically based, that is to say they rely on data rather than theory to inform. Some place the emphasis on classificatory systems or typologies, and others such as Finkelhor's framework (discussed later) incorporate other theories into the model. The interest in typologies for perpetrators has fluctuated over the years: the belief that incest offenders represent a distinctly different clinical problem from paedophiles (extra-familial offenders) was seriously challenged by research in the 1980s (most notably Abel et al., 1987) which identified a high level of cross-over between sexually deviant behaviours. Similarly, Groth, Hobson, and Gary's model (1982) of a dichotomous classification between fixated and regressed perpetrators has been criticised for being overly simplistic and inaccurate: they described the fixated offender as having a primary and fixed erotic interest in children, usually males and of early onset; the regressed offender has a primary erotic interest in his peers, and the sexual abuse, usually against female children, is episodic and occurs in response to stress. It has been suggested however (Salter, 1988) that a deviant pattern of sexual arousal may be a crucial differentiating factor between types of perpetrator, regardless of the sex of the victim or their relationship with the perpetrator.

Perhaps the most sophisticated empirical classification typology for perpetrators is the model proposed and refined by Knight and Prentky (1990) and Prentky, Knight, and Rosenberg (1988). Their rigorous analysis of a large sample of perpetrators yielded two axes: Axis 1 involves a dichotomous rating on two dimensions, degree of fixation on children, and social competence; Axis 2 consists of a hierarchical series of decisions involving the amount of contact with children, the meaning of the contact to the offender, the degree of physical injury, and the presence of sadism. The system appears to be reliable and the subtypes stable, and the authors assert that considerable explanatory power and possibly predictive power will be sacrificed if perpetrators are considered a homogeneous group. Nevertheless, further research work needs to be completed in order to reduce the number of possible combinations from 24 (in which 11 cells hold a very low frequency of subjects) to a more practical level.

The Challenge Project (Craissati & McClurg, 1996, 1997), in assessing their 80 subjects, used chi-square analysis to examine the variables associated with possible types of perpetrator. Two significant subgroups emerged, distinct but overlapping: the first related to men with a history of sexual victimisation (52% of the sample), who were significantly more likely than non-sexually victimised subjects to have:

1. abused male children
2. committed the offences of anal intercourse
3. abused a greater number of victims
4. admitted to experiencing deviant fantasies

5. experienced emotional difficulties and abuse as children
6. engaged in sex play with boys as children
7. self-harmed and received psychological help as adults
8. engaged in sexual contact with other men.

The second subgroup related to men with previous sexual convictions (31% of the sample), who were significantly more likely than subjects without previous sexual convictions to:

1. use physical coercion against the victim
2. abuse the victims for a shorter period of time
3. abuse strangers/acquaintances
4. be single
5. have had contact with psychological services as an adult.

Whilst the second group could be seen to represent classically paedophilic patterns of offending, the first group suggested that childhood sexual victimisation might play a central role in shaping markedly disturbed psychosexual development. Both recidivism and childhood sexual victimisation were found to be important contributors in predicting the failure to comply with treatment (see Chapter seven).

Perhaps the most popular multi-factorial model amongst current practitioners is Finkelhor's 4-factor framework (1984, 1986) in which to organise the various theories explaining child sexual abuse. Finkelhor aims to account for the diversity of abusive behaviour by emphasising the complementary, rather than competing, nature of explanatory models:

Factor 1: Emotional Congruence.   Emotional congruence refers to the way in which children have some especially compelling emotional meaning for many perpetrators. This factor includes the role of low self-esteem and feelings of social inadequacy in accounting for relationships with children which bring feelings of power, omnipotence and control; perpetrators with a history of sexual victimisation may seek mastery of their own trauma through repetition and identification with the aggressor.

Factor 2: Sexual Arousal.   The research on experimental evidence for unusual sexual responsiveness to children in these perpetrators is complex; generally, there is evidence for heightened deviant sexual arousal for extrafamilial perpetrators but the evidence is much less clear for incest perpetrators. A history of childhood sexual victimisation is often put forward as evidence that the deviant sexual interest has been conditioned or modelled by early sexual experiences. If early arousal is incorporated into a repeated masturbatory fantasy, it is likely to be highly reinforced over time.

Factor 3: Blockage.   Blockage refers to theories which address why some individuals are blocked in their ability to meet their sexual and emotional needs in adult heterosexual relationships. Developmental blockage relates to perpetrators who cannot relate appropriately to their peers for reasons of poor social skills, sexual anxieties, or more profound disturbances in relation to theories of primary object relations and oedipal conflicts. Situation blockages relate more to incest theories where a perpetrator with apparent adult sexual interests loses his normal sexual outlets because of a transitory crisis or loss of a relationship.

Factor 4: Disinhibition.   Normal inhibitions against having sexual contact with a child are either overcome or not present in perpetrators: the two empirically supported factors are alcohol—which is highly likely to be implicated in offending behaviour—and the "incest avoidance mechanism": the increased risk that a stepfather poses to a child because of different norms or different exposure to the child at an early age which relaxes control over the incest taboo.

Typologies provide helpful classificatory systems with the potential to predict treatability and recidivism, and to help in making difficult decisions regarding resource allocation or public safety. However, as descriptive models, they have no explanatory power and should be studied in conjunction with one of the prevailing theoretical models set out in the following pages. A multi-factorial framework such as Finkelhor's provides an essential summary of most of the theoretical and empirical approaches to child sexual abuse, usefully separated into meaningful categories. However it loses much of the richness of single-factor perspectives with its emphasis on descriptions of "how" and not "why" men become perpetrators. Nevertheless, for those who already have a clear theoretical understanding of aetiology, the framework provides a clear indication for the focus of possible therapy, and the range of ideas which need to be explored.

PSYCHODYNAMIC THEORIES

Psychoanalysis, as a developmental theory, has attempted to provide a complex aetiological account of adult sexual interest in children, which has to be extrapolated to some extent from general analytic theories of perversion. Perversion, in its general usage, is a pejorative term which is, however, used by analysts specifically to denote the sexualisation of the aggressive instinct: in perversion there is the characteristic of repetitive fixed behaviour—a sexual act which is insistent and gratifying—which leads potentially to orgasm, "the erotic expression of the sexual deviant is an essential feature of his psychic stability and much of his life revolves around it" (McDougall, 1972). Howells (1981) describes three main themes in the analytic literature:

1. Perversions such as paedophilia occur in the context of avoidance of anxiety-laden heterosexuality (Glasser, 1990).

2. The identification of important non-sexual components in deviant sexual behaviour, such as the coping and mastery functions wherein fantasy and/or behaviour is rewarding because it induces a sense of control, competence or dominance (Rosen, 1979; Stoller, 1975).
3. The paedophile's involvement with children occurs in the context of an idealisation of the characteristics of childhood.

However all analytic approaches would agree that a detailed account of the paedophilic act is essential, including the circumstances leading to it, as it lays out a map of the individual's specific psychopathology.

For Stoller (1975) the perverse fantasy or act is a defensive cognitive structure which acquires its gratificatory powers through its capacity to serve as a scene of symbolic mastery over childhood-induced psychological traumas. An essential element in most perverse fantasies is that they involve a symbolic "act of revenge". These ideas were developed by Rosen (1979) in his account of perversion as a regulator of self-esteem: he described the preservation of the personality as an integrated whole, as one of the functions of self-esteem, whose regulation is essential to healthy psychic functioning. A poor self-image and weak masculine identity may render the individual vulnerable to repeated humiliations in latency and adolescence; perverse fantasies and behaviour serve to raise his sense of self-worth, secured by his capacity for active conscious control of his perversion. Running risks introduces the element of excitement which raises self-esteem.

Both Rosen and Glasser detail the early formative experiences of the perpetrator in relation to his primary objects, which they believe to be commonly found in the perverse individual, and in paedophiles in particular. Typically mothers are experienced (although not necessarily reflecting reality) as both seductive or intrusive, and depriving or threatening to the boy's unfolding masculinity, usually because they relate to their children in terms of their own needs; as the needs of the infant's self are not recognised, the mother is experienced as annihilatory (or fundamentally threatening to the sense of self). Fathers play a crucial role in the development of the perversion, in terms of their emotional absence (and sometimes physical absence) or open hostility to the child; father's adequately masculine presence is essential to protect the boy against mother's anxieties, and for the boy to develop his own full masculinity. The final form which the perversion takes is determined largely by chance external events which occur later in childhood, particularly in adolescence, when orgasm further establishes the object and nature of the sexually deviant act. In this way, later experiences of sexual abuse, rejection, humiliation, and perhaps comforting sexual experiences with peers play an important role in behavioural terms.

Perhaps one of the most central analytic models currently used in relation to the perversions, and adult sexual interest in children in particular, is the "core complex" (Glasser, 1979, 1988). In its simplest form, it is accessible to the non-analytic practitioner, and may provide a useful framework for understanding the perpetrator with a persistent sexual interest in children. Glasser details three stages in the core complex:

1. The paedophile has a conviction that the person who is the object of his most intense emotional longings (mother) threatens to possess and thus annihilate his separate identity.
2. As a consequence he reacts with a withdrawal from objects, resulting in a situation of total emotional isolation, with feelings of complete abandonment and consequent low self-esteem. The intense misery of deprivation prompts the longing for a complete union with the object.
3. The second consequence is the self-preservative aggression felt towards the object—an essential part of the ego's response to any threat to physiological or psychological homeostasis—which would result in the destruction of the object. This irreconcilable internal conflict leads to the sexualisation of the aggression, converting the intention to destroy into the wish to hurt and control (sadism). The paedophile's ultimate defence against the object is the perverse act: involving his penis he asserts his masculine separateness, devaluing the object; the relationship is intense but real intimacy can never be present. Sadism or hostility may express itself subtly in the perpetrator's dealings with children, or more obviously in what he inflicts on the child in the course of the abuse; he attributes to the child painful and shameful childish feelings, then derives profound gratification from his role as caring and benevolent parent, transforming into a cruel attacking and envious parent with some feelings of triumph. If the process of sexualisation diminishes or breaks down, sadism may revert to aggression.

This model may best be demonstrated by a case example:

Eric described an intense relationship with his "devoted" mother; he never knew his father who had abandoned the family early on, and was only referred to with contempt by his mother and grandmother. His mother occasionally brought Eric into her bed at night when she felt low, pushing him out again without explanation; she was also prone to retiring to her room with mysterious illnesses, becoming unavailable to him, causing him anxiety regarding her apparent fragility. During his pubescent years, Eric was sexually victimised by a friendly older man who introduced him into his circle of young male victims; this was an experience he found immensely gratifying—although confusing. As an adult Eric was fearful of women, and was encouraged by his mother to remain at home. Apart from some unsuccessful heterosexual encounters, Eric's main sexual outlet was masturbatory fantasies of boys. Two years after his mother died, and after a period of depression, Eric began to offend sexually against a young male neighbour, whom he described as ". . . cheeky, arrogant, one of the boys . . . everything I never was . . . I was fascinated by the tight bulge in his trousers . . .". He maintained that they were equals, ". . . more than equals; he twisted me round his little finger, I offered him pocket money but he always wanted more, he'll get into serious trouble one day."

From this example, it is possible to identify components of the core complex in terms of Eric's experience of an intrusive but sometimes rejecting mother and the absence of a strong male role model leading to poor individuation and masculine self-image. There is evidence of withdrawal from adult relationships into a world of fantasy as a means of avoiding engulfment or the expression of dangerous negative feelings, but this solution failed when his mother died and unbearable emptiness ensued: Eric then sought out an alternative—but safer—relationship with a boy over whom he could exert control. His description of the abuse suggested feelings of envy and longing towards the victim whilst retaining control and mastery of the situation—at least initially—until his desire to be close to the boy was increasingly superseded by an aggressive denigration of the victim's character and behaviour, triumphantly predicting the boy's downfall.

The question of incest has been less closely observed by psychoanalysts, although Glasser (1988) is at pains to point out that abuse within the family should be differentiated from paedophilia on the grounds that the former manifestly transgresses the incest taboo and involves intense intra-familial dynamics; Gaddini (1976) suggests that incest represents a longing by the perpetrator for a second chance to achieve a symbiotic contact which had never been achieved with his mother.

Family systems therapists have attempted to incorporate issues which involve the individual, extending their concern to the family and the social context, into a single conceptual context. Observations of the family have been based on the premise that a system (or family) can be defined as an organised arrangement of elements consisting of a network of interdependent coordinated parts that function as a unit. The presenting symptom—for our purposes, child sexual abuse—is considered in terms of its importance and power in stabilising family life and the degree to which, in turn, it is maintained by family dysfunction. Bentovim (1996) outlined the descriptive terms which describe family patterns, including affective life, communication patterns, boundaries, alliances, adaptability, and stability of organisation and competence.

Both Bentovim (1996) and Furniss (1991) discuss families where child sexual abuse has occurred in broadly two main typologies: conflict-avoiding and conflict-regulating families. Furniss refers to the primary confusion between hidden conflicts on emotional and sexual levels between the parents. The secondary process is that which maintains the abuse, where the child is locked into sexual abuse with the father on the basis of threats and mutual guilt, and the mother and child's development of trust is blocked by feelings of rejection or guilt, leading to secrecy. Ultimately, there is a confusion of hierarchies within different levels of practical care, emotional care and sexual partnership between the parents, and between each parent and the child. The result may be that family members are caught up in a collusive system in which sexual abuse can continue for a long time.

Conflict-avoiding families are described as highly enmeshed with an intense over-involvement between father and daughter, and a more distant and hostile relationship between mother and daughter; conflict between the parents is avoided because of fear that it would result in destruction and breakdown, and the sexually abusive contact often emerges out of a long-standing sexual failure in the marriage. Mother and daughter appear to be very dependent on father, there is intense secrecy and poor communication regarding sexual matters in the family. The discrepancy between the family's self-image and the reality of the quality of actual family relationships is marked, and they may appear to be well functioning, governed by strict moral family rules. Child sexual abuse serves as a means of denying emotional/sexual imbalance and tension between the parents, the child is placed into a pseudo-adult sexual alliance with father, and mother is excluded by secrecy.

Conflict-regulating families are more likely to present with chaos and poor care, with weak boundaries both between generations and individuals; violence and punitiveness often emerge in communication patterns and marital conflict, even violence, may be openly visible; alliances may shift and involve more than one child as a victim of abuse and/or in the parental position. The child may be surrendered to the father with relatively more open knowledge, but the major secrecy is between the family and the outside world. Child sexual abuse provides an outlet for father's aggression, reduces marital conflict which could lead to family break up, and the collusion between the parents increases father's dependence on his wife who tolerates the abuse and keeps him emotionally bound to the family.

There is a considerable body of work relating to the psychoanalytic understanding of deviant sexual interest, although theoretical conclusions have often been drawn from atypical subjects, biased sources and small numbers. Furthermore it is only relatively recently that they have taken into consideration definitional problems such as the need to develop psychologically meaningful subcategories of child sexual abuse (Howells, 1981) which take account of factors such as victim age, degree of aggression displayed, fantasy versus behaviour, and gender of perpetrator. There are a number of difficulties in extrapolating from a comprehensive aetiological model to a focus for therapy: the intransigence and primitive nature of the defence mechanisms utilised means that even when the small number of highly motivated paedophiles seek psychoanalytic-based therapy, they are extremely resistant to change. Treatment is slow and expensive in terms of resources, and the training requirements are rigorous. Nevertheless, it can provide the practitioner with an important understanding of the sado-masochistic dynamics that are so often played out in all forms of therapy with this client group.

Models of incest often appear to spread responsibility for the abuse across family members, failing to appreciate legal and child protective aspects to the problem, and as such rest uneasily with practitioners who struggle to manage denial and justifications in their clients. Nor does a systemic model aim to provide a causal, rather than descriptive model, for perpetrators can often be seen to be powerful in shaping the dynamics in their family. The clear description of families is perhaps at its most constructive when families wish to be rehabilitated, and practitioners are concerned with communication patterns, prognosis, child protection, and risk prediction.

COGNITIVE–BEHAVIOURAL MODELS

There are a number of theoretical approaches which could broadly be described as behavioural in orientation, and in fact many overlap with or are subsumed within multi-factorial models. The decision to focus on the predominantly cognitive–behavioural approaches—epitomised by the sexual assault cycle (Ryan, Lane, Davis, & Isaac, 1987; Wolf, 1985)—is based on the current prevalence of this model in providing the core of treatment programmes.

Behavioural theory was based on two principles of animal learning, derived from empirical studies—classical, and operant conditioning—which provided an explanatory model as to why behavioural responses could initially be conditioned and subsequently maintained by reinforcement. Developments over time introduced the concept of loosely linked response systems: behavioural, cognitive, affective, and physiological; and attention gradually shifted to cognitive attributes, developed by Beck (1976). The key cognitive concepts relevant to a consideration of sexual offenders are schemas or core beliefs, underlying assumptions, and automatic thoughts. Schemas are stable cognitive patterns which develop in early life as part of normal cognitive development, and are shaped by events and relationships; underlying assumptions are conditional beliefs based on schemas (for example, if "I am unlovable", then "anyone who gets close to me will reject me"); automatic thoughts are the cognitions that automatically and temporarily flow through one's mind and will often reflect persistent cognitive distortions. Schemas are a powerful mechanism in maintaining problems or distortions because they determine what an individual notices, attends to and recalls of his experiences.

Both Ryan et al. (1987) and Wolf (1985) refer to the importance of childhood sexual victimisation in developing a learned response which is repeatedly reinforced; Ryan described its impact in terms of "either a learned helplessness or a repetitive aggressiveness". Wolf stated that the abused child "would enter adolescence and/or adulthood with a lower baseline of resistance/sensitization to deviant attractions . . . when under stress, the clients' responses will include using sexuality to self-gratify and to avoid dealing with the attendant stressor". Ryan does broaden her consideration to exposure to inappropriate sexuality or attitudes, and to loss or betrayal in the preverbal years.

Wolf describes the early experiences as potentiators because of their influence on later attitudes and behaviours. Disinhibitors are defined as transitory environmental factors, or internal states, which play an important role in weakening the inhibition against and strengthening the attraction to sexually deviant behaviour.

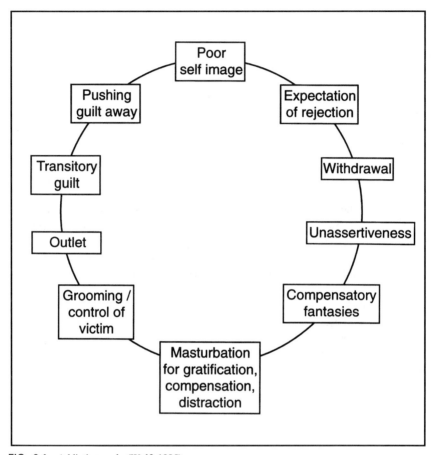

FIG. 2.1   Addiction cycle (Wolf, 1985).

Both authors emphasise the reinforcing nature of sexual behaviours, and Wolf pays considerable attention to the function of masturbatory fantasy. Masturbation acts as a disinhibitor towards the behaviour fantasised about, it reinforces the attraction towards the fantasised behaviour, and it reinforces the rationalisations and justifications used in the fantasy. The fantasy itself is a cognitive rehearsal of deviant behaviour, and as such begins to shape the individual's environment. Fantasy recognises the victim as a potential sexual partner, and incorporates perceptions (distortions) of the victim's behaviour which feed the potential perpetrator's own justifications for the choice of victim, and give him permission to act out sexually.

Wolf's addiction cycle (Fig. 2.1) traces the cognitive, affective, physiological, and behaviour components of sexual offending, and is similar to the cycle described by Ryan et al. (1987) which they use with adolescent perpetrators.

Poor self image (the underlying schema) leads to an underlying assumption that intimacy brings rejection; social withdrawal is one coping response, but subsequently isolation and feelings of inadequacy are redressed through compensatory fantasies, which take on a sexual tone often related to someone in the immediate environment; distortions creep into the fantasy to give permission for acting out; guilt is usually related to fear of being caught, rather than the offending behaviour itself, and needs to be denied by reassurances that minimise what occurred and insist it will never happen again.

The strength of these approaches is the detailed consideration of fantasy, arousal and planning in sexual offending, and the clear cyclical structure which an offender may follow once, or repeatedly. There are strong resemblances to psychoanalytic thinking—albeit couched in different language—reminiscent of the phases of the core complex. However, the cognitive–behavioural model provides an accessible backdrop to a clearly formulated therapeutic intervention which lies within the grasp of a broader range of practitioners. Unfortunately, there is an inadequate elaboration of why childhood experiences of physical or emotional abuse only should lead to the development of deviant sexual fantasies; why many victims of childhood sexual abuse do not become perpetrators; what determines whether a perpetrator offends against a child or an adult; and how the cycle might explain the behaviour of intra-familial offenders who may demonstrate little or no deviant sexual arousal.

This review of the main theoretical approaches to perpetrators of child sexual abuse has been selective and, inevitably, simplified. As the models are scrutinised, it can be seen that there are considerable overlaps in their core concepts, and a working knowledge of all the models is advised in order to develop the breadth of understanding necessary for careful assessment and treatment.

CHAPTER THREE

Assessment

The assessment of perpetrators of child sexual abuse does not begin and end with the initial interview but is an ongoing process, repeated throughout a perpetrator's sentence, treatment, and/or involvement with social services. Most practitioners will be familiar with the need to examine the relevant documents, and to take a detailed personal and offence history. Superficially, assessment may appear to be a straightforward affair. However, the complexities of understanding the aetiological factors underpinning the offending behaviour, the unreliability of self-report, and the uncertainties of estimating risk combine to make assessment a skilled task, requiring theoretical knowledge, training, and experience. It is important to bear in mind that assessment is an intervention in its own right; the perpetrator's experience of the interview will have a significant impact on his willingness to contemplate his behaviour as problematic, and on his ability to engage constructively in treatment with the assessor or with another agency at another time. Managing perpetrator denial is a central issue, and will be addressed fully in the subsequent chapter.

REASONS FOR ASSESSMENT

In referring a perpetrator for assessment, agencies may have different expectations or concerns which will not always be explicitly stated. If a court report is required, for example, there will be an expectation that aggravating and mitigating circumstances are outlined, that there is an assessment of risk and perhaps recommendations for disposal, including a consideration of treatability. Social services may refer an alleged perpetrator for treatment, but subsequently request for a risk assessment, which may have serious consequences for the therapist–client relationship, particularly if legal proceedings ensue. Indeed assessments for social services perhaps pose the greatest professional and ethical dilemmas because an expert's opinion may have immediate and marked consequences for the perpetrator and the children in the family. It is preferable that at the outset, the reasons for the referral are clarified and, other than in exceptional circumstances, a comprehensive assessment made. This will normally include:

1. An analysis of the offending behaviour and the perpetrator based on a multi-factorial model of child sexual abuse.
2. An assessment of the estimated risk of future reoffending based on established recidivism research.
3. Recommendations for risk management, including treatability.

Although agencies may vary in their primary roles, assessments are made with the overriding objective of protecting children.

At this stage, it is important for the assessor to consider (1) whether she is qualified to complete the assessment; and (2) whether there are personal/ethical barriers to the completion of a valid assessment. Personal experiences of sexual abuse, close involvement with the victim, abhorrence of sexual offending, or an established therapeutic relationship with the perpetrator are some examples where strong emotional or professional alliances may interfere with an assessment.

SOURCES OF INFORMATION

All forms of assessment suffer from problems of reliability, whether it be self-report in interview, behavioural observation, questionnaire, or psycho-physiological measures. In all but exceptional cases, the perpetrator will wish to present a favourable impression which minimises the extent of his destructive and abusive behaviour. There are no infallible means for overcoming these difficulties, but expending considerable effort in accessing relevant documentation and liaising with other agencies involved, will help to minimise the difficulties. Crucial documentation will include:

1. social services case conference reports
2. probation reports ("pre-sentence" and/or "home circumstances")
3. previous psychiatric/psychological reports
4. a list of previous convictions
5. the witness statements (Crown Prosecution evidence).

To some extent the victim statements—if sufficiently detailed—will provide an adequate victim perspective with which to inform the assessment and avoid collusion with the perpetrator. Direct contact with the victim, either in video interview or in person, can be problematic, both because it may interfere with the criminal proceedings, but also because it is likely to evoke a strong emotional reaction in the assessor which may result in an overtly or covertly hostile interview with the perpetrator. Maintaining a facilitative stance in interview will help to manage denial.

Communication with key professionals further aids the gathering of accurate information, which sometimes may be poorly recorded in the available documentation. Constructive working relationships reduce the risk of polarisation where agencies act out the perpetrator–victim dynamics in relation to each other, viewing each other as alternately collusive and hostile. It also establishes a norm for future communication should the perpetrator enter treatment.

The assessor may wish to consider contacting a key informant, usually a family member, who might be able to offer corroborative information. Information acquired in this manner should be interpreted with caution as the family member is likely to be emotionally involved in the outcome—positive or negative—for the perpetrator. Nevertheless, informants may be able to add a useful perspective, for example, on the circumstances and stressors in the perpetrator's life at the time of the offending behaviour.

PSYCHOMETRIC MEASURES

There are two types of psychometric measure which may assist in the assessment of perpetrators: the first are questionnaires, and the second is the penile plethysmograph (PPG)—a physiological measure of sexual arousal.

Questionnaires

Self-report questionnaires may provide the assessor with useful additional or corroborative information. Ideally, scales should be chosen which have been carefully standardised, and provide comparative information or scores for the normal population and other sex offender populations. They should have established reasonable levels of reliability and validity, and are particularly helpful when they have been adjusted for social desirability bias, alerting the assessor to attempts to fake good or bad, or a propensity for psychological denial. Where normative data are available, comparisons can be made in the scores, or pre- and post-treatment comparisons can be made. In this instance, caution should be applied in interpreting the scores, as an apparent deterioration—for example in cognitive distortions—may indicate a greater truthfulness as a result of treatment. Indeed, questionnaire results should always be treated circumspectly: their focus is often transparent and they are vulnerable to faking; some are phrased in a complex manner and utilise sophisticated language which may prove difficult for perpetrators of low intelligence. They should never be used as a substitute for skilled interviewing.

There are many questionnaires available which may be relevant to this group of sexual offenders. Some suggestions are outlined below—those that were used in the evaluation of the Challenge project—and they are reproduced in Appendix II with normative data where available. Although well known, the Abel and Becker Cognitions Scale was subsequently dropped by the project because of its excessive transparency. The following are probably the most frequently used scales (see Beckett, Beech, Fisher, & Fordham, 1994; Craissati & McClurg, 1997; Salter, 1988), although rather dated; it does take time for new scales to establish relevant normative data and practitioners should regularly review published scales in order to update their evaluative process.

Attitudes towards Women (Spence & Helmreich, 1972, 1978).   This 15 item scale rates respondents' views towards various aspects of women's role (vocational, educational, intellectual, and interpersonal relationships), ranging from "conservative" to "liberal".

Fear of Negative Evaluation (Watson & Friend, 1969).   This 30 item scale rates respondents' sensitivity to criticism, and their avoidance of situations in which such criticism is possible.

Buss–Durkee Hostility Inventory (Buss & Durkee, 1957).   This 66 item scale rates respondents' general anger and hostility. It can be broken down into seven subscales: negativism, resentment, indirect hostility, assault, suspicion, irritability, and verbal hostility.

Interpersonal Reactivity Scale (Davis, 1980).   This 28 item scale rates respondents' capacity for general empathy, and contains items related to both cognitive role-taking and emotional responsiveness.

Multiphasic Sex Inventory (Nichols & Molinder, 1984).   This 300 item questionnaire produces 20 clinical scales and a sexual history. They include scores on validity (psychological denial, distortions, and justifications), sexual deviance (cognitions and behaviours thought to be common to child sexual offenders), atypical sexual behaviours, sexual dysfunction, sexual knowledge, and treatment attitudes.

Penile plethysmograph

The PPG is a laboratory-based technique for directly measuring penile tumescence in response to a range of auditory and visual stimuli. These stimuli may include a range of subjects, both male and female, from children to mature adults, and may portray varying degrees of coercion, threat, and seduction. The perpetrator's sexual response is then compared to his reaction to consenting sex between adults.

Despite its clinical and research value, particularly in differentiating the sexual preferences of child sexual abusers, it has never been as widely used in Britain as in the United States for example. The equipment is expensive and requires skilled administration and considerable expertise in interpreting the results. A large body of research has produced strong—but not infallible—evidence to suggest that the PPG is useful in demonstrating clear sexually deviant interest in some child sexual abusers, particularly extra-familial abusers (see Murphy, Haynes, and Worley, 1991, for a broader review of the literature). However, the PPG is a test of an individual's sexual preference; it cannot determine whether an individual has acted or will act on it. Langevin (1988) elaborated on some of the problems associated with interpreting PPG results, including questions regarding the validity of the stimuli, the influence of anxiety and/or prolonged sexual abstinence on arousal and attempts at conscious repression or distortion of arousal. Nevertheless, where a deviant arousal pattern is found, it can be effective in helping challenge those offenders who deny their guilt.

THE CLINICAL INTERVIEW

The clinical interview lies at the heart of any assessment. The time available may be restricted to some extent because of resource limitations and impending deadlines. The assessor will be concerned to gather the maximum information as efficiently and effectively as possible. To this end, there are three types of information which are distinct but inter-related:

1. Factual information gathering. This includes the establishment of "who, when, why, what and where", and is of course subject at times to problems of self-report.
2. Qualitative information gathering. This relates to the perpetrator's perception of the "facts", the way in which he experienced and now reports the events of his life and his offending, offering clues into his inner world. The assessor should be prepared for impoverished or concrete responses and may need to probe specifically for qualitative answers.
3. Your experience of the perpetrator in interview. The ease with which you establish rapport, the perpetrator's response to gentle challenges, his level of arousal—sexual and aggressive, the depth of affect, your feelings about him; may contribute to an understanding of the degree of psychological disturbance, and possible response to treatment.

The assessor will need to decide the order in which to gather information. Some may prefer to commence with the offence details, as this clearly establishes the purpose and agenda of the interview. The difficulties in doing so are considerable as the perpetrator will immediately be on the defensive, and may well have prepared a number of evasive and exasperating responses which lure the assessor into a confrontational stance. It may be more productive to commence with the background history, or perhaps to offer the perpetrator the choice of where to start. Gathering a personal history at the outset will have the dual benefit of enabling the perpetrator to feel he is being considered as an individual, and help the assessor to develop greater empathy with him before broaching the offending behaviour.

The following areas of focus cover the predominant themes of assessment.

Setting the scene

It is important at the outset to establish the framework of the assessment. Whilst being professionally appropriate, this stance will also help to establish an open, collaborative dialogue with the perpetrator. The framework should include the following.

Who you are.   The perpetrator should be informed about your profession, the agency you work for, and your relationship with the other agencies involved.

Reasons for Assessment.   As detailed above, the perpetrator should be clear about what information will be covered, and the purpose for this. It is helpful to give an indication of the duration of the assessment and whether questionnaires will be used.

Confidentiality.   There is a tendency for clients in distress to forget the limitations of confidentiality, and to relate to an empathic assessor as though, for example, consulting with their general practitioner. It should be made clear from the beginning that all relevant information will be recorded in a report, and to whom the report will be sent. This is particularly important when the perpetrator is pleading not guilty to some of the charges against him. Furthermore, if questionnaires are used, it is essential to clarify whether they are for treatment/ research purposes only, or whether the results will be included in the assessment report.

Sources of Information.   The perpetrator needs to know what documentation is available to the assessor and with whom she is in contact.

Feedback.   Assure the perpetrator—whenever possible—that the outcome of the assessment and the recommendations made will be fed back to him at the end of the interview. Normally it will be appropriate for the perpetrator to see your report eventually.

Acknowledgements.   It is crucial to acknowledge that the perpetrator is facing a life crisis at the present time, facing the possible breakdown of his family, loss of employment, and probable imprisonment. The offences are of an extremely shameful nature and discussion of them will cause acute embarrassment. It may help to pre-empt some degree of offence denial if the interviewer is prompt to predict the perpetrator's wish to minimise their behaviour as a natural tendency of individuals in his position who wish to give a good impression of themselves. Ironically, it can be explained, this may have the opposite effect, arousing the suspicion of the professionals involved and the hostility of the court.

Childhood and the family of origin

The early experiences of the perpetrator form the core of his personality development and are the basis on which later relationships are likely to be modelled; there are likely to be long-term emotional consequences as a result of extreme or prolonged deprivation, separation or trauma early in life.

1. Who was in the family, and whether there were any losses or separations (including placement in care).
2. Description of mother and father (or other key figures) and their relationship with the perpetrator and with each other.
3. Experiences of violence or emotional abuse in the family, and the perpetrator's understanding of why this occurred.
4. Serious illness or hospitalisation as a child.
5. Evidence of childhood behavioural or emotional disorders, their cause, duration and consequences, including referral for specialist help.
6. Forensic, substance misuse, and psychiatric history in family members.

The following is an example of how persistent questioning might be required in order to elicit interesting information (from an assessment session with **Kevin**).

A: Perhaps you could tell me something about your family.
Kevin: There's not much to tell, it was a good childhood.
A: Tell me something about your mother, as she was when you were growing up.
Kevin: She was OK . . . what would you like to know.
A: Describe what she was like as a person, to give me a picture of her.
Kevin: She had long legs and silky hair down to her waist . . . she used to call me the man of the family.
A: And your father?
Kevin: I only met him twice, he was in the Army.
A: What was your impression of him?
Kevin: The first time, he went straight up to the bedroom with mum and they locked the door—I only saw him on the way out. The second time, I saw him in the street and he walked the other way.
A: How did you feel at the time?
Kevin: Nothing, I didn't know him anyway.

Educational, occupational, and social history

Educational difficulties may reflect or exacerbate early emotional difficulties, leading to poor self-image, difficulty in managing the workplace and social isolation.

1. Academic interests and performance in primary and secondary schools.
2. Learning difficulties or special schools.
3. Behavioural problems at school including truanting (alone or with others), fights, suspensions/expulsions.
4. Being bullied or being a bully, including details.
5. Evidence of aggression or delinquent behaviour outside of school (alone or with others).
6. Quality of social integration with peers, including intensity of relationships.
7. Employment history, including stability of work record and reasons for dismissal/redundancy.
8. Is there a discrepancy between apparent ability and achievements?.
9. Evidence for work or socially related contact involving child-centred activities.
10. Degree of isolation in adulthood, capacity for social integration.

Psychosexual history

The aim is to trace sexual development with regard for the symbolic importance it plays in personality development, providing information directly relevant to considering risk and treatability.

1. History of his own experience of sexual victimisation, if possible detailing the perpetrator, means of seduction, nature of the physical acts, his feelings and thoughts at the time, whether he disclosed it and if not, why not, and the longer-term impact of the experience as he views it in retrospect.
2. His sexual learning experiences, including unusual and peer sexual encounters, the role masturbation and fantasy played in his early childhood, adolescence, and adulthood and the degree to which he was preoccupied by it.
3. Exposure to and use of pornography, and how often used.
4. History of sexual encounters and relationships, choice—and gender—of partners (age and other characteristics), difficulties in the relationships and reasons for breakdown, including details of any violence, sexual dysfunction, sexual dissatisfaction and sexual encounters outside the main relationship.
5. History of unusual sexual outlets such as cross dressing, voyeurism, or sado-masochistic practices.

Tom (who was himself grossly sexually abused by his step-father over many years as a young child) reported the following psychosexual history:

Eventually Tom anticipated his father's sexual abuse with some relief "... I knew that if he came to my room at night, I wouldn't get a beating the next day ..." When he was 15, he was thrown out of the home and this was how the abuse stopped. However in order to fund his drug-taking, and for more ambiguous reasons that he was unclear about at the time of assessment, Tom began soliciting in public toilets, and worked occasionally as a male prostitute. He had a number of sexual relationships with women, and viewed himself as predominantly heterosexual (seeking out brief homosexual encounters when he wished to be buggered, as a source of comfort when very low in mood). During both his long-term relationships, he sought out women who might let him down, and quickly felt used by them which served to justify his anger, controlling behaviour, and occasional serious violence towards them. Eventually he admitted to the use of coercive and humiliating sexual fantasies during sexual intercourse with his partners, which intensified as he became increasingly intimate or dependent on them.

Adult mental health problems

Information on adult mental health problems will guide the interviewer on considering mental fragility, suitability for treatment, and the need to draw in other resources.

1. History of self-harm, frequency and severity.
2. History of "nervous breakdown" and the nature of it, psychological or psychiatric out-patient or in-patient treatment, use of prescribed medication.
3. History of illicit drug use, type, duration, and frequency.
4. History of alcohol use, including social, heavy, and dependent drinking.

Offending history

This is perhaps the most important area in assessing risk and providing an overview of the pattern of offending.

1. Nature of previous non-sexual offending, with particular regard to the motivation for offending, frequency, and circumstances.
2. Nature of previous sexual offending, the details of which should be gathered as recommended for "Details of index offences"; it is particularly important to explore whether there is a pattern of escalation over time or a cross-over between type of offending or choice of victim.

Details of index offences

Detailed information may be difficult to gather at the assessment stage if the perpetrator is in denial and the witness statements are not particularly informative; however it can lay the foundation for future treatment directions and may demonstrate someone's capacity to think about his offences and their triggers.

Precursors to the offending. These may sometimes be difficult to disentangle from emotional and interpersonal distress subsequent to the onset of the offending behaviour.

1. Evidence of increased anxiety or depressed mood, duration and intensity.
2. Life events and stressors, for example loss of employment (financial problems), bereavement, divorce (or significant marital discord and estrangement), sexual problems, particularly impotence, work pressures, illness, family tensions.
3. Recourse to heavy consumption of alcohol.

Victim.

1. Gender, age and relationship to perpetrator.
2. Specific characteristics, including vulnerabilities as viewed by assessor, and by perpetrator.
3. Evidence for a link between victim characteristics and perpetrator's own childhood experiences.
4. Details of victim's disclosure and its consequences.
5. Quality of perpetrator's relationship to victim, including capacity for caring, ability to view child as separate individual, or as a rival for the affections of the mother.

Behaviour.

1. Minute details of the offending behaviour—"what did you do?"—to the extent that he is willing and able to provide the information.
2. The progress of the offending, the way in which it began, whether opportunities were created, the duration, frequency, and whether it escalated; what attempts were made to stop, degree of risk taken.
3. Evidence for making the victim "special", bribery, covert or overt verbal threats, violence.
4. Awareness of, or ability to describe thoughts and feelings at the time of the offending.

Example of assessment interview with **George**:

George had already begun to acknowledge the egocentric nature of his "love" for John, who he had abused on a weekly basis between the ages of 7–12. He felt that John had attracted him because he was good looking, athletic and popular, and cared for by his parents—he had everything George lacked himself as a child. It was also relevant perhaps that he was the same age as George was when first abused. Only in retrospect could he understand that it was only his excessive bribery of John that maintained the abusive relationship, and that when he was unavailable to him, he sought out a younger cousin as a replacement, both temporarily and for the future when John reached puberty and was no longer attractive to him. George experienced the sexual contact as utterly compelling, and obsessive to the point of desperation. His contact focused on John's penis as though it was able to "give me something I never had". He never felt satisfied afterwards, and would frequently masturbate to deviant fantasies inbetween encounters. George was aware that he was taking increasing risks—masturbating John while his parents were in the car with them—to the point where he appeared to be begging to be caught. When finally arrested, George disclosed the abuse fully, in far greater detail than the allegations against him. He experienced an enormous sense of relief, went home, took a potentially lethal overdose of tablets, but was discovered by an unexpected visitor.

Cognitive distortions   (see Chapter four for further details on eliciting distorted attitudes and beliefs).

1. Explore and differentiate between superficial distortions related to a defence against feelings of anxiety and guilt, and more pervasive and deeply held beliefs or schemas, which are probably related to developmental experiences which have created the foundation for distorted beliefs regarding children and sexuality in adulthood.
2. What are the characteristics and behaviours of children which trigger the distortions.
3. Do certain moods or situations increase the likelihood of a distorted view.

Examples of cognitive distortions might be:

"... girls are sexually precocious these days and I know she was sexually active.."
"... she acted all flirty, she knew exactly what she was doing"
"... he knows his own mind, if he didn't like it, he would've told me."
"... we were friends, it was a mutually loving relationship ... something special, the sex thing was just a small part of it ..."

Arousal and fantasy.

1. Degree to which he was physically aroused and masturbating before, during or after the offending.
2. Onset of sexually deviant fantasies, and whether they have been persistently experienced, and masturbated to, throughout adolescence and adult life.
3. Does denial of deviant sexual fantasies suggest conscious or subconscious lying, or is there such an impoverished fantasy life that it is the offending which provides the only fantasy material.

4. Degree of preoccupation with victim and sexual fantasy maintaining the offending behaviour.
5. Degree to which he relates fantasy material with ease or even excitement.

Example of assessment interview with **Kevin** when he had been denying any sexual content to the offending:

A: Once you started abusing Sally, I would imagine it played on your mind a lot of the time.
Kevin: Yes, I suppose it did.
A: Would it be fair to say you became quite preoccupied with her and the incidents of abuse.
Kevin: I couldn't get it out of my mind.
A: Did she always feature in your fantasies when you masturbated during this period?
Kevin: No not always.
A: But sometimes?
Kevin: Yes.
A: I know that many men in your position have struggled to let go of these fantasies once they have been caught and the abuse is over. Let's talk about how you have been trying to control your sexual thoughts.

Consequences.

1. Behaviour when interviewed by police, denial or cathartic confession.
2. Suicide attempts, persistent suicidal ideas, severe depressive illness, or incapacitating anxiety (requiring psychiatric referral).
3. Plans, if relevant, to be rehabilitated with family.
4. Attempts to contact the victim.
5. Threats from the family or immediate community.

Formulation of the problem

Perhaps the most taxing aspect of assessment is the collation and summarising of the material gathered, so that the "story" can be given a coherent framework. Formulation, in the clinical sense, provides the bridge between the assessment and decisions about therapy; furthermore it is possible that decision-makers (such as the judiciary, and parole board) will only refer to the conclusion and recommendations in a report. In terms of perpetrators of child sexual abuse, it may be helpful to refer to a framework containing three principal factors (see Fig. 3.1) in order to formulate the problem. Vulnerability factors refer to those experiences—internal or external—which may shape the nature of the perpetrator's personality, his behavioural, emotional, or relationship difficulties, and his potential to become an abuser. Triggering factors refer to events and behaviours which may reactivate early trauma and/or reduce inhibitions to offending.

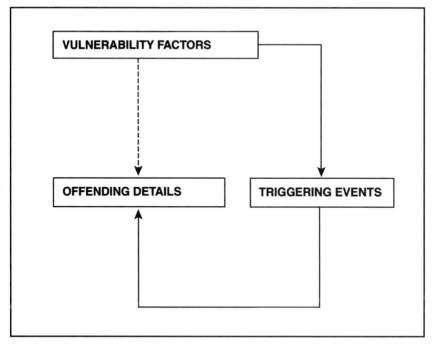

FIG. 3.1 Formulation of the problem.

Offending factors refer to aspects of the sexual offending which are potentially significant, and may give clues as to the thoughts and feelings underpinning the offending behaviour. The three factors never operate in isolation from each other, although different perpetrators may require greater or lesser emphasis on one factor.

The case studies:

Tom's background was characterised by profound emotional, physical, and sexual abuse at the hands of his step-father; he resented his mother's emotional withdrawal and failure to protect him. His only source of "affection" was his stepfather's sexual abuse which, over time, he learnt to look forward to and enjoy. He learned that sex was a source of comfort, where relationships brought pain, and that if he could be controlled by it, so could others. In adult life, Tom sought out women who might let him down, thus justifying his anger towards them and avoiding intimacy and painful rejection (**vulnerability**). Mary's mother was a vulnerable woman, whose difficulties with parenting the children served to emphasise Tom's own mother's failures. He alienated his wife by his behaviour, then focused on her "betrayal" of him as justification of her "sluttish" unreliability. When she left, and he had sole care of his daughter, her availability provided the opportunity to take both the brief comfort of sex, and to seek revenge (**triggers**). The offending behaviour was characterised by overt violence and conscious elements of sadism towards Mary, whereby Tom revelled in her fear and his control of her. "I wanted to take back what had been taken from me". Although Tom presented with intense feelings of self-disgust and low levels of denial, it was often unclear in interview when he was talking of the offence and when of his own victimisation experiences, thus suggesting that emotionally he continued to operate as the abused and raging child (**offence**).

Peter's background details were vague: he appeared to have had distant parents who worked hard and failed to set boundaries for his behaviour, thus leaving him mainly in the company of other boys. He was forced to perform oral sex in the park on one occasion by a drunken woman, but denied any feelings of fear or disgust. He developed a friendship with a much older boy, who encouraged him to talk about sexual fantasies of girls at the swimming pool. These two sexual experiences appear to have been crucial in the development of his fixed deviant sexual interest in prepubertal girls (**vulnerability**). He underachieved in his employment and developed an anti-social career which ran parallel to his sexual offending. Alcohol was the only significant identifiable precursor to the index (and previous) offending: the degree of intoxication appeared to be correlated with the degree of violence and impulsivity manifested in his sexual assaults (**triggers**). Peter's presentation in interview was striking for the richness in detail of his offending behaviour—as outlined in reports and his self-disclosure—in comparison with the barren quality of personal and emotional details. He was clearly aroused by discussing his fantasies and perverse behaviour, but had no understanding of why his offences might be harmful; his detachment regarding his previous victims mirrored his own parents' apparent detachment towards him (**offence**).

George's background was one of emotional deprivation: his mother—whom he had perceived as a "slut"—abandoned him when he was eight; his father was a heavy drinker, emotionally distant and overly punitive towards him. His seduction into a child pornography ring provided him with a form of loving and parenting which was absent at home, and sexualised companionship with another, adored, boy. He learned that his penis was much admired and sought after, and the source of all comfort to him. Nevertheless, he was brutally assaulted by the "mother" of the family and developed high levels of anxiety when with women (**vulnerability**). George persisted in his sexual interest in prepubescent boys, but lost the opportunity to have sexual contact after he left school. The index offences began after he moved closer to John's family, bought his own home, and began working shorter hours. These changes appeared to have been driven by increasing feelings of isolation and loneliness, and fading fantasy material from his own childhood (**triggers**). John was a target because "he had everything I never had as a child". George truly believed that they had a "man and wife" relationship, refusing to recognise the bribery involved in seducing John, and the compulsively sexual nature of their relationship. His risk-taking whilst offending appeared to represent a need to disclose which was related to his own childhood victimisation, and led eventually to a cathartic confession to the police. It was this disclosure which appeared to facilitate a slow return to "reality" and the ability to distinguish between his distorted appraisal of his own childhood experiences, and the almost delusional quality to his perception of his offending behaviour (**offences**).

Kevin's background was discontented but not unduly abusive. His mother was an attractive woman, apparently concerned with her appearance; his father was in the Army and did not live with them, visiting perhaps twice during his childhood. Kevin's relationship with his mother was rather enmeshed with distorted mother–child boundaries: she referred to him as the "man of the house" and he saw himself as her companion in life. Nevertheless she had the occasional lover, and on one occasion he bitterly recalled being locked out of the house whilst his parents were in the bedroom. He was a shy child, self-conscious about his illegitimate status and his appearance, and badly bullied at school as a result. His tentative attempts to form heterosexual relationships in adulthood resulted in rejection and humiliation, and he withdrew socially (**vulnerability**). Eventually he came to the rescue of a woman battered by her previous partner, and moved in to the household where her mother and her 11-year-old daughter also lived. There was considerable conflict in the relationship because—from Kevin's perspective— his partner's mother was "an interfering old witch"; his partner took on a part-time evening job which exacerbated Kevin's feelings of insecurity, and it was at these times that he babysat for Sally (**triggers**). Kevin presented Sally as sexually precocious and seductive, clearly in control of the situation (although he acknowledged that as an adult he should have resisted); he began to allow her treats and to talk to her as a peer. Once he had initiated sexual contact, he became totally absorbed by the contact and it rapidly escalated over the four month period, in parallel with the deterioration in his relationship with his partner. Sally disclosed once the adults had separated (**offences**).

RISK FACTORS

The term "dangerous" is all too often applied to sexual offenders, implying as it does a stable, internal personality trait which is unaffected by external or internal circumstances, such as relationship difficulties or periods of emotional instability. Risk, as a concept, allows us to move away from the pejorative and emotional connotations associated with "dangerousness", towards an assessment based on predominantly empirical data. Furthermore, perpetrators within our current social and political system are likely to remain in or return to the community, and as such have to be managed. Treatment is one form of risk management.

One of the failures of risk assessment is the lack of clarity in defining the task. It is highly pertinent to clarify what you are being asked to predict, all offending behaviour for example, or just sexual reoffending; the time scale involved is highly pertinent as some perpetrators may only reoffend every 10–20 years; it may be

TABLE 3.1
Factors significantly predicting the risk of sexual reconviction

Static factors	Dynamic factors
Male victims	Laboratory measured deviant
Number of prior sexual offences	sexual arousal
Younger at conviction for first sexual offence	Alcohol abuse
Single	Problems in establishing
Sociopathic traits	meaningful relationships
Use of force during offence	with adult
Number of previous victims	
Intercourse during offence	
Low intellect	

important to distinguish between the likelihood of an offence re-occurring, and the severity of any reoffending, in terms of harm to the victim (including the possibility of escalation); the assessor must take into account known base rates for the predicted behaviour (that is the frequency with which it occurs in the general or offending population), as cautious practitioners tend to overpredict risk, the number of false positives raising difficult ethical considerations; clinical interviews can provide important additional information, but subjective impressions can never take the place of assessments based on known predictive factors derived from research evidence (Campbell, 1995); extraneous factors such as the degree to which the offending violates social norms, the penalties it accrues, the aversive experience of prison and personal consequences such as the loss of family, may all play a part.

Despite methodological problems, there is a body of research evidence now available which can usefully guide risk assessment. Much of this data is based upon sexual reconviction rates, which should not be confused with the consideration of treatability. Quinsey, Lalumiere, Rice, and Harris (1995) reviewed 17 independent research samples, comprising a total of 4483 perpetrators of child sexual abuse, and highlighted the differences in recidivism rates between studies probably related to differing study and sample characteristics, and length of follow-up. They found that the weighted average sexual reconviction rates was 20.4% ranging from 4% to 38%. When the data were analysed by gender and victim–perpetrator relationship, they found the following sexual reconviction rates: incest offences only, 8.5%; female victims, 18.3%; male victims, 35.2%.

This would appear to suggest that offenders against boys, and offenders against children outside of the family tend to have higher sexual reconviction rates. It is probable that this differing pattern of reconviction rates is fairly representative of the pattern of reoffending rates (most of which do not lead to detection or reconviction).

In drawing out the factors which have been identified, variably, by the studies in significantly predicting the risk of sexual reconviction, they can be summarised as shown in Table 3.1.

TABLE 3.2
Algorithm for risk classification based on record data
(Fisher & Thornton, 1993)

RISK FACTORS
- any previous sexual convictions
- 4 or more previous convictions of any kind
- any current/previous conviction for non-sexual violence
- convicted of sexual offences against 3 or more distinct victims

Number of risk factors present	Risk classification
0	low
1	medium/low
2	medium/high
3 or 4	high

It is important to note that there is little evidence as yet to link dynamic factors such as denial and victim empathy to rates of recidivism, despite being the primary focus of treatment these days (Hanson & Bussiere, 1996; Quinsey et al., 1995).

Thornton and Travers (1991) in a longitudinal study following up convicted sexual offenders found that simple prediction scales could categorise "higher" and "lower" risk groups of sex offenders. This work was subsequently presented as an algorithm for risk classification based on record data (Fisher & Thornton, 1993) and is outlined in Table 3.2.

In terms of the case studies, the risk assessments were summarised as follows:

Tom was assessed as posing a medium to low risk of sexual reoffending according to the algorithm (scoring 1), but he nevertheless posed some concern to the Project—the offences had contained considerable overt aggression and he clearly had relationship problems—but violent (non-sexual) reoffending appeared to be as likely, given the pervasive use of violence in all relationships and an earlier history of anti-social behaviour.

Peter was assessed as posing a high risk of sexual reoffending (scoring 3 on the algorithm), despite the relatively minor nature of his index offence. He clearly articulated a persistent deviant sexual interest (not laboratory tested), he had a number of prior sexual convictions involving violence and penetration and commencing at a young age, he had been dependent on alcohol for many years, and had an earlier history of antisocial behaviour. Externally driven motivation to abstain from reoffending was fuelled by his knowledge that future reconviction would result in an extremely long prison sentence.

George was assessed as posing a low risk of sexual reoffending (scoring 0 on the algorithm), but this was amended to moderate in order to reflect the pervasive and long standing nature of his deviant sexual interest: his victim was male, and his sexual interest in boys commenced at a very young age;

he also had relationship problems which had only recently improved. The risk was perhaps mitigated by his clear distaste for his offending behaviour and his terror of losing his new family.

Kevin was assessed as posing a low risk of sexual reoffending (scoring 0 on the algorithm) as he presented with only relationship problems as a negative predictive factor. The threat of prison was a considerable additional deterrent.

Having completed the assessment, including a clear formulation of the problem and a consideration of the risk factors involved, it remains to consider plans for management. Where a perpetrator is utterly resistant to acknowledging any involvement in offending behaviour whatsoever, then options are clearly reduced, and child protection concerns become the primary focus. However, for perpetrators who are convicted by the courts, and for some less resistant offenders who are refered via health or social services, treatment becomes one of a range of management options. The subsequent chapters aim to address this area.

CHAPTER FOUR

Managing denial

Denial probably poses the single most important challenge to practitioners working with perpetrators of child sexual abuse. One common assumption made about sex offenders is that full admission at the assessment stage will more probably lead to treatment success because the perpetrator can confront the realities and consequences of the offence and understand the underlying motives or predisposing factors to the offending behaviour. Yet such an expectation can only lead to disappointment and undue pessimism.

Denial is exemplified by discrepancies between the offender accounts and the witness statements in a prosecution case; it may lead to considerable additional trauma to a victim who has to give evidence in court, and undoubtedly longer custodial sentences for the perpetrator as a result; it provides a reason for excluding perpetrators from treatment in some contexts, and is equated with lack of motivation to change. For practitioners, denial poses an emotional obstacle course which evokes overwhelming feelings of rage, revulsion and a compelling need to retaliate against the perpetrator: denial will be poked, prodded, dissected, stripped bare and, if necessary, detonated, in order to elicit an admission approximating to the "truth". It is sometimes difficult to understand how a perpetrator can be driven to such lengths in order to deny some aspect of his offending behaviour, and convoluted explanations can appear to have a delusional quality to them in which all reality testing is kept at bay. For example, perpetrators have alleged in interview how "the guilty plea for buggery was entered whilst I was asleep in the dock"; that "I'm a collector—of stamps—and having completed my collection of Luxembourg, I thought, what next? Why not child pornography?"; and for an elderly man convicted of taking indecent photographs of a four-year-old girl's bottom and anus, "she bent over and begged me to do it . . . what could I do? . . .".

Denial is not a single state, and indeed becomes a much more manageable concept if broken down into components which may lie along a continuum. Most work on sex offender denial has highlighted three key components: denial of the behaviour; denial of responsibility; and denial of seriousness. A review of the authors' observations is detailed here.

Kennedy and Grubin (1992) interviewed 102 convicted sex offenders in prison regarding their attitude to their offences. A cluster analysis revealed four sub-groupings: (1) "rationalisers" who admitted their offences but denied causing any harm to their victims. They were the most recidivist group and offended against children, particularly boys; (2) "externalisers" blamed the victims and spouses for their offending, and felt persecuted by the criminal justice system. They contained a significant number of recidivists, and predominantly offended against young females; (3) "internalisers" readily admitted to the offences and accepted harm to the victim although they viewed their behaviour as a temporary aberration out of keeping with their normal character. They reported high levels of distress and had offended mainly against female children within the family; (4) "absolute deniers" were mostly convicted of offences against adult females and included at least 75% of offenders from ethnic minorities in the sample.

Matthews (1991) reported on patterns of denial in incarcerated sex offenders as part of the Prison Department initiative to establish nationwide treatment programmes for sex offenders. He identified eight denial strategies: (1) total innocence—involving a conspiracy or mistaken accusation; (2) no offence committed—they were present at the scene but nothing untoward occurred; (3) no memory—acceptance of guilt but no recollection of the actual offence; (4) inexplicable outburst—some unfortunate combination of circumstances/unique stress gave rise to the single, unplanned, never to be repeated, offence; (5) external factor—acceptance of guilt but no acceptance of personal responsibility as it is not part of their usual behaviour and there were external (alcohol, family, injustices, unemployment) stresses; (6) guilty but harmless—admission of offending and responsibility, but no harm to willing victim as a result; (7) reformed—acceptance of offences but mitigating factors involved (led on, temporary misjudgement, happened a long time ago) and now a reformed character; (8) admits—admits to behaviour, responsibility and seriousness of offending.

Salter (1988) breaks denial down into: (1) denial of the acts themselves, in which she includes family denial and the offender's inability to perceive himself as a child molester, minimisation of the extent of the behaviour; (2) denial of fantasy and planning, when the degree of deviancy is not acknowledged; (3) denial of the seriousness of the behaviour and need for treatment, including harm to the victim, or the need to think about what happened, or religious/moral conversion as a substitute for treatment; (4) denial of responsibility for behaviours blaming drink, spouse, work, loneliness; (5) full admission with responsibility and guilt.

Salter goes on to describe the perpetrator who genuinely does not deny as the individual who admits the extent of his deviant sexual interest; his story of the abuse matches that of the victim; he is able to describe previous thoughts and fantasies, the planning of the offence and the seduction of the victim; he is able to identify potential triggers to relapse and understands the uncertain nature of psychological change; he feels guilty for his behaviour and knows the harm it has caused. In other words, the perpetrator who does not deny is the perpetrator who has successfully completed treatment (or the psychological processes akin to treatment).

UNDERSTANDING DENIAL

Psychodynamic theories classically understood denial as a primitive mechanism of defence; an attempt to disavow a present existence of reality (Stevenson, Castillo, & Sefarbi, 1989), in which determinants of motivation are primarily unconscious and therefore inaccessible to the individual (Rogers & Dickey, 1991). Such motivations may symbolise impending psychotic disintegration or be used to ward off overwhelming anxiety. Examples of such defence structures might be found in those fixated paedophiles who insist that their 'love' for the victim has been misrepresented and distorted, and whose denial allows them to maintain in fantasy a relationship with an idealised object, an identification with themselves as a child. However, as Stevenson et al. (1989) point out, the offence is often fully present in the mind of the denying sexual offender and may not involve a primitive unconscious set of internal defences. Suppression may offer a more apt alternative definition which refers to the conscious inhibition of an impulse or a feeling, as in the deliberate attempt to forget something and put it to the back of one's mind. It may be that some father figures, who minimise the abusive behaviour and project the blame for the offence onto the victim, are attempting to deny their own sexualised feelings towards the child which are unacceptable to them given their parallel desire to be a "good and loving parent".

If unconscious denial and supression lie on a continuum, then the next stage prior to admittance, may be Rogers and Dickey's (1991) adaptational model, derived from Rogers' work on malingering: the adaptational approach is based on decision theory which postulates that the choice of malingering (or denial) is based on expected utility. The sexual offender, when confronted, almost always perceives himself to be in an adversarial setting in which he will lose by self-disclosure and gain by denying; feigning or denying in these instances may be perceived as a more effective (or the only alternative) strategy for achieving his goal. In support for this strategy decision, Craissati (1994) found that in southeast London, it was always advantageous to a perpetrator to plead not guilty to charges of rape or buggery against a child; even if found guilty at trial, they received shorter sentences than perpetrators who made full admissions of penetration from the outset. Further research (McClurg & Craissati, 1997) revealed that judges were increasingly inclined to ignore recommendations for community treatment and impose custodial sentences for offences of indecent assault against children, even when other pertinent variables were controlled for.

Whether unconscious, semi-conscious or a deliberate strategy, the primary function of denial is self-protection: it enables the perpetrator to preserve an acceptable self-image which is not contaminated by negative perceptions such as "pervert", "homosexual" or "sexually inadequate"; it protects him from uncomfortable feelings of guilt and self-denigration; it may help to deflect violent reprisals away from himself, and spare him and his family the wider shame which follows admission; specifically and crucially, the perpetrator may fear the disintegration of key personal relationships if denial is not maintained. This is supported by anecdotal evidence that death or abandonment by a key emotional figure—usually wife or mother—often leads to a breakdown of denial in the perpetrator. In this sense, denial in the early stages of abuse disclosure may have a positive function for the perpetrator in that it allows for a period of adjustment for the individual (and perhaps his partner), so that in time other less radical defences may be mobilised.

> **George** was a perpetrator whose motivations, initially, for denying the reality of his behaviour appeared to be grounded in unconscious processes: his blindness towards the abusive nature of his behaviour towards John enabled him to maintain a fantasy of having been loved and parented himself by his own sexual abusers in childhood; all feelings became sexualised and he was unable to perceive the anger and revenge contained within his controlling and humiliating offences. The interview with the police appeared to be a turning point, in which he made an extensive cathartic confession, followed by a potentially lethal suicide attempt; this appeared to be motivated by conscious feelings of shame in relation to family and friends who had no idea of his "secret life", and by a despair at the instantaneous loss of his "lover". It seemed as though his own disclosure to the police—revealing, as it did, his parallel existence—symbolised an unconscious need to disclose his own victimisation as a child. Aspects of his denial began to seep into his conscious mind and to be discarded—over a period of a few years—until he was ready to enter therapy. At this stage, he was able to present a reasonably open and realistic picture of his offending behaviour, but continued to suppress the most uncomfortable aspects of his feelings: his longing for his mother to love him, the way in which he was used and discarded by his substitute paedophilic parents, and the emptiness which such feelings brought.

MOTIVATIONAL INTERVIEWING

Motivational interviewing (MI) is an approach originally developed in work with problem drinkers (Miller, 1983). It is an interviewing style which can be used to help clients identify, explore, and possibly resolve ambivalence about a problem behaviour. The aim is to activate and consolidate motivation to decide to change. The emphasis must always be on the client—not the worker—expressing concerns about the problem behaviour and to express arguments for change. A key text for further reading is Miller and Rollnick (1991).

More recently, the MI model has been applied to sexual offenders whose behaviour has been likened to other "addictions" (that is, repetitive, self-reinforcing behaviours), and a detailed exposition of this work is usefully outlined in the NOTA publication, Motivational Interviewing with Sex Offenders (Mann, 1996). Beckett (1994) has summarised the goals of MI as:

1. anticipating offender resistance
2. maximising offender cooperation
3. establishing a non-collusive, collaborative relationship.

and he outlines two basic assumptions to the adapted model:

1. Denial is constructed by the perpetrator during the course of the abuse to help minimise guilt and anxiety.
2. Interview strategies which moderate fear and anxiety lessen the need for such a defence and increase the likelihood of engaging the offender in constructive dialogue.

The Stages of Change Model (Prochaska & DiClemente, 1982; since modified) provides a structure in which to understand the motivational cycle which individuals pass through—once or repeatedly (Fig. 4.1).

Clearly sex offenders who deny aspects of their offending behaviour can usually be located at the stage of "pre-contemplation" or "contemplation". In the former case, the task for the practitioner is to raise doubt in the perpetrator's mind by increasing his perception of risk and problems with the abusive behaviour. In the latter case, the practitioner wishes to emphasise reasons to change, strengthening the perpetrator's belief that he is able to do so, and thereby tipping the balance in favour of a decision to take constructive action.

There are five principles of motivational interviewing (Mann, 1996; Miller & Rollnick, 1991):

1. Express empathy: which is communicated through the skill of reflective listening, with the firm understanding that ambivalence is normal.
2. Avoid arguments: and even direct persuasion in order to evade being trapped in a confrontation-denial discussion.
3. Roll with resistance: resistance is an expression of ambivalence, not a personality characteristic.
4. Deploy discrepancy: ambivalence is characterised by a lack of discrepancy between what the individual is doing and what he wants to do; motivation

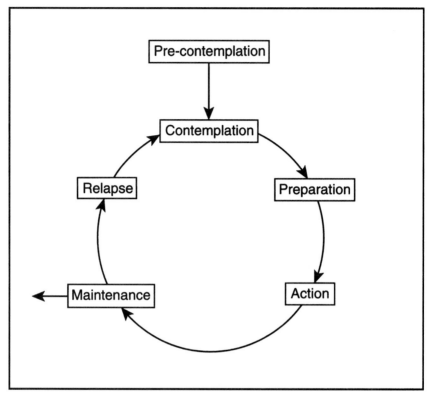

FIG. 4.1   Stages of change model (Prochaska & DiClemente, 1982).

develops as a sense of discrepancy between present behaviour and important goals is created.

5. Support self-efficacy: demonstrating belief in the possibility of change, and eliciting and reinforcing clients' own problem-solving strengths.

It is important to emphasise at this point, that many of the interviewing methods recommended by motivational interviewing authors reflect standard, high quality therapeutic skills which many experienced practitioners will intuitively deploy with perpetrators. For example, the use of open questions and reflective listening will be familiar to many, although all too often, the skills required are underestimated. With sex offenders, reflective listening can be used to selectively ignore or emphasise aspects of a perpetrator's response to an open question; to reinforce certain elements of what has been said, or to reframe or summarise the answer and in doing so, alter its meaning slightly. At all times, the interviewer is concerned to elicit and reinforce self-motivating statements which approach some recognition that there is a problem, some expression of concern, and any intention to change or optimism about change.

Undoubtedly, punitive impulses on the part of the interviewer when faced with an irresponsible, unrepentant, evasive perpetrator can be overwhelming. It may be difficult to identify—outside of supervision—when a challenging remark has entered the domain of a punitive remark, or when the necessary exploration of offending behaviour in a group setting has become persecutory. Practitioners fear that failure to confront cannot be separated from a collusion with the perpetrator; that empathy and understanding will be understood as condoning. The following quotes are extracts from conversations with experienced practitioners or from reports to the courts, and give some indication of the potential difficulties that interviewers can themselves perpetuate.

Express empathy: "... he was more concerned with feeling persecuted by the Courts than with the impact his behaviour may have had on the victim ..."

If the traumatic experiences of the victim are put to one side momentarily, there can be few experiences so humiliating for a hitherto "law-abiding" citizen than to be convicted of a sexual offence against a child: his behaviour is detailed in court, his family, friends, local community and employment are all likely to know something of what has occured, and he faces the unknown fear of custody as a "nonce". Few strategies are more effective in setting a constructive tone to an interview than in responding empathically to the perpetrator's current situation.

Avoid arguments: "... she says you had intercourse with her, and a victim never lies ..."

There are two difficulties to this stance; firstly, although victims rarely lie, they may be confused, have poor recall or exaggerate occasionally, and such a debate with a perpetrator can take the the interview down an unconstructive path; secondly—and more importantly—the perpetrator is, in essence, being called a liar, and such an approach is likely to activate his most defensive stance.

Roll with resistance: "... his attitudes are distorted and he denies responsibility for the offence, therefore I would not consider him to be treatable ..."

Here, denial has been mistakenly labelled as a stable personality trait, rather than a strategic manoeuvre, consciously or unconsciously designed to protect the perpetrator from the anxiety engendered by feelings of shame and guilt.

Deploy discrepancy: "... how can you possibly call youself a loving father when you abused your son? ..."

In responding with indignation to a perpetrator's claims to have cared for his victim, the interviewer has lost a prime opportunity to emphasise the discrepancy between the perpetrator's caring feelings and his abusive behaviour, which could have enhanced his perception of concern or risk. This statement could also have been understood in terms of seriously undermining the perpetrator's feelings of self-worth (this is discussed later).

Support self-efficacy: ". . . once a sex offender, always a sex offender . . ."
". . . simply avoiding children in the future is hardly going to reassure the probation service that you no longer a risk . . ."

Both these statements, implicitly or explicitly stated, demonstrate the interviewer's pessimism regarding the intentions and potential for change in the perpetrator. There can be few greater barriers to engagement in treatment than a sense of inevitability regarding reoffending.

The following examples from interviews with perpetrators attempt to demonstrate the motivational interviewing approach (some of the dialogue has been condensed).

Extract from initial interview with Kevin

K   I recall the night I touched her vagina . . . and rubbing myself against her when we were watching television . . . but I don't remember the other incidents she mentioned.

Th   So you are aware of two incidents but not of the three others Sally details which she said occurred over a six month period. (*Reflecting both perspectives.*)

K   Yes, I don't remember them at all . . . she said different things to her mother and later to the police . . . the story kept changing.

Th   It seems that you have a strong sense that Sally was lying. (*Amplified reflection to elicit ambivalence.*)

K   No, no, she's not the sort of girl who lies, I'm just saying that I don't recall what happened.

Th   So, you feel that Sally is probably telling the truth, that these incidents probably occurred, but you feel very vague yourself about the details. Do you have any thoughts about why these incidents are so unclear in your mind? (*Paraphrasing and reframing memory loss as "unclear".*)

K   I was drunk for much of the time, I know that . . . lots of things happened which I can't remember, I'm not responsible for my behaviour after a certain amount of alcohol.

Th   Yes, many people suffer from memory loss when their drinking becomes out of control, but with time you will find that the memories return, and until then, we can perhaps rely on the witness statements for guidance regarding what occurred. (*Agreement with a twist.*)

From the above example, Kevin could be described as one of Kennedy and Grubin's (1992) "externalisers", relying on "external factors" and the "no memory" strategy outlined in Matthews (1991). The therapist has attempted to explore the discrepancy between the perpetrator and victim accounts of the abuse, without directly confronting him on his evasions. Many perpetrators will withdraw from a direct allegation that the victim is lying, particularly if they have had a relatively warm relationship together prior to the abuse. Empathic concern for Kevin's alcohol misuse and consequent memory loss allowed for the issue to be reframed in terms of a temporary lack of clarity regarding recall which clearly stated the therapist's agenda whilst allowing Kevin to maintain his denial strategy in a revised form.

Earlier in interview, Kevin had been quite distressed when questioned:

K I looked after Sally better than her real dad ever did, and we had lots of fun together . . . I don't know why she's said all these hateful things about me, it's all been distorted.

Th It must be terribly difficult to come to terms with the fact that you could be such a loving father figure and yet hurt her so badly by your behaviour.

In empathising with this positive aspect of his personality—which was not refuted in the victim statement—Kevin's self-esteem is not threatened, and yet the therapist has managed to enhance discrepancy between his desired role as father, and his destructive role as abuser.

Perpetrator A

Mr A received a two year custodial sentence and was being interviewed with a view to treatment upon release.

A It was a one-off, I must have been out of my mind. He was right to tell his mum of course, I've got what I deserve—punishment. I've learnt my lesson.

Th It seems that it felt to you that you suddenly lost all control of yourself, and you feel very badly about it now. (*Reflection with amplification and naming the feeling.*)

A Yes, but I've put it all behind me, I've learnt my lesson.

Th Perhaps you can tell me a little more about what you've learnt from the experience. (*Elaboration.*)

A Well . . . I know it won't happen again.

Th From what you've said, it sounds as if you are someone who normally stays calm and in control of your behaviour.

A Yes I am, certainly.

Th Well, it would be helpful, I think, to explore what unusual circumstances led to this sudden loss of control. (*Elaboration looking back.*)

A It just happened, there was no build up.

Th You mean it felt like an impulsive action that came out of absolutely nowhere. (*Amplified reflection.*)

A Pretty much, I mean I was under stress at the time, but that's no excuse.

Th Tell me about the stresses in your life at that time.

. . . (later in interview) . . .

A I told the probation officer that I have been punished by the courts and there's no need to go to a group. She says that sex offenders reoffend, but I know I won't.

Th   Well, you are right, of course in one way, not all sex offenders reoffend, but it is sometimes quite difficult to know who will and who won't. People want proof which you're unable to give. (*Confirm self-efficacy but agreement with a twist.*)

A   Yes, I know I don't intend to reoffend, but they don't believe me.

Th   I do recognise that you have taken the very important step of openly declaring your sincere intention never to assault a child sexually again. It takes a good deal of courage simply to admit that it happened in the first place. I wonder how we can take this a step forward. (*Confirm self-worth and shift to looking forward.*)

A   Well I need to prove to others that I'm no longer a risk.

Th   I wonder what options might be available to you to help you do that. (*Explore goals.*)

Mr A could be described as an "internaliser" using a "reformed" denial strategy. The therapist has allowed him to maintain his resistance against being labelled as a sex offender, but has attempted to highlight any discrepancies in his account. Notice how effective even slight exaggerations in reflection can be in triggering a revised stance from the perpetrator. The therapist has managed to develop a very empathic mode of responding to Mr A which, at no time, has colluded with his miraculously "reformed" strategy.

Interview with Mr B for court report

Five minutes into the interview:

B   I just want to point out that there are loads of inaccuracies in her statement . . . OK, things got out of hand, but the lies and exaggerations make me mad. I held up my hands to the first charge, but the others are crap—excuse my language—I only pleaded guilty to save her having to be humiliated in court. Let me tell you what happened . . .

Th   (interrupts) Mr B, please let me stop you there for a moment. I should say that the only things I know about you are contained in the prosecution documentation and relate to the offending. Obviously that gives me a limited understanding of who you are and what has happened in your life. I would like to start with some background details, and we can come back to the offences at the end. (*Affirmation.*)

B   Sure, where do you want me to begin.

. . . (later in interview) . . .

Th   . . . which leads us to the point at which your feelings towards Lisa became sexual.

B   It wasn't as bad as she made out . . . she makes me sound like some creepy scheming little nonce.

Th   I can understand that reading the witness statements makes you feel very uncomfortable. (*Reflecting feelings.*)

B   Too right, I couldn't recognise myself.

Th It must have been a shock to compare who you believe yourself to be, with what you have done to Lisa, as though there are two completely unrelated sides to yourself ... (silence) ... I understand from your Proof of Evidence—your formal statement—that you have challenged any allegations of penetration. Have I understood that correctly? (*Clarification.*)

B   Yes, she ...

Th (interrupts) So perhaps we could leave those matters to one side, and focus on those areas of Lisa's statement that you do accept—those aspects of your behaviour towards her which prompted you to plead guilty to the first charge. (*Highlighting possible avenue of problem recognition and expression of concern.*)

Mr B clearly presented initially as an angry man who wished to control the direction of the interview. The therapist decided on a strategy which would take back control of the interview—interrupting him and setting the agenda—without entering into a destructive (and exhausting) confrontation-denial trap. This decision was based on the assumption that Mr B's anger and need for control were possibly not stable personality traits, but rather an aggressive defence against shame and anxiety. Returning to the theme of his offending behaviour, he was much more amenable to an empathic reflection of his feelings. Once again, the therapist chose to interrupt him before he could retreat into well rehearsed denial strategies, and clearly reformulated the problem to focus on his area of lowest resistance.

Initial interview with Peter

P   I admit it of course, I have strong sexual feelings towards young girls, but this time nothing happened, nothing sexual I mean.

Th Tell me more about your perspective of what did occur. (*Elaboration.*)

P   Well, her parents were friends of ours and—like many times before—we were round there, and I was mucking about with Rosie, she liked to wrestle. She was in her nightie and I suppose she told her mum something about our games. The fuss is all about nothing.

Th But, although you feel the fuss is all about nothing, or very little, nevertheless the impact on you and your family has been devastating—here you are in prison again, social services are involved and questioning your family, and your wife can't cope. (*Emphasising the two sides of the ambivalence.*)

P   I get so frustrated just sitting here, twiddling my thumbs and unable to help my wife fight off social services ...

Th It is difficult to have so much time to think (*paraphrasing*) ... one of my thoughts is how come someone of reasonable intelligence like yourself, with three previous convictions for serious sexual offences against children, could allow yourself to wrestle—however innocently—with a 5-year-old girl. (*Enhances discrepancy.*)

P   Well when you put it like that, you're right really, it was stupid, I'd been so careful for the past six years.

Th   Careful to control your sexual feelings and sexual behaviour—and with some success since you stopped drinking so heavily. Perhaps it would be fair to say that you could only have behaved so rashly if you had begun to develop a sense of sexual excitement when mucking about with her. (*Suggestion in the context of reflecting self-efficacy.*)

P   I suppose it's possible.

Th   That your self-control was beginning to slip . . . which leads us to the question of where do we take this next. (*Shifting from problem recognition and concern to thoughts of change.*)

P   I want to go on the programme you offer, I can handle prison of course, it has no impact on me, but I've never had treatment in the past—it was never offered—and now's my chance.

Th   You are keen to seek treatment, which would suggest that you feel there's a problem to work on. Can you say a bit more about that. (*Elaboration of self-motivational statement.*)

P   Well, I don't want to offend again, I want to get control of my impulses, make something of my life, a chance that no-one's ever given me.

Th   This offence does appear to have happened as a result of loss of self-control and you feel treatment would give you an opportunity to improve your impulse control and set appropriate goals for the future. (*Agreement with a twist.*)

Peter is able to relinquish much of his resistance when he receives positive feedback regarding his attempts at exerting self-control over recent years. The therapist is able to selectively ignore his attempts to blame others for the fuss, interference and lack of help (although it is often a mistake to refer to social services as this usually triggers an unreasonable tirade of abuse towards them from anxious perpetrators). The therapist has made potentially threatening suggestions, only when framed within empathic or affirming phrases, and has focused upon self-control as a key motivational statement. In fact Peter's motivation for treatment is uncertain, as he is a "rationaliser", unperturbed by incarceration or potential harm to victims, but the therapist has rephrased his superficial motivation to include a clear statement that he has reoffended and that the key to treatment lies within himself.

Undoubtedly the perpetrator of child sexual abuse presents a challenge to practitioners in terms of assessing the nature and quality of denial, and making decisions regarding possible treatment approaches as a result. Even the most sophisticated techniques and experienced interviewers will fail to engage some perpetrators, which leaves practitioners with feelings of frustration and the uncomfortable awareness that it may only be time—and another offence—which shifts such attitudes. Nevertheless, perpetrator denial must be placed within the context of normal human behaviour: people do not generally offer full and truthful accounts of their sexual fantasies and behaviour on request; when an individual's self-image is threatened, they often resort to denial and projection of blame; most offenders before the courts make calculated decisions regarding their pleas and the quality of their admissions; sexual offenders are the most despised and condemned of all offenders; and there is little to gain in the present social climate from full admission. It is the acceptance and acknowledgement of these factors by the practitioner which begins the process of building empathic rapport with a perpetrator and maximising the fullness of their disclosure.

CHAPTER FIVE

Parameters of treatment

There are a range of considerations to be taken into account before embarking upon a treatment programme for perpetrators of child sexual abuse, which could be broken down into three general areas: constraints, management and practice, and clinical decisions.

CONSTRAINTS

Enthusiastically implementing intensive treatment programmes from the United States must be tempered with a careful appraisal of the aims of the local service, client needs, and the practitioner's role in the organisation. Resource limitations, a preponderance of one type of perpetrator, or the potential therapists' skills may exert more influence in shaping a treatment programme than books and articles. Nevertheless, if resources are limited, it is all the more important to design efficient and efficacious interventions; this may involve decisions regarding the length of a programme, the number of people admitted to a group, excluding some "barely treatable" perpetrators from intensive interventions or alternatively targeting higher risk perpetrators only.

For example, a fairly simple dilemma may be posed if an anti-discriminatory policy states that only two or more black perpetrators will be put in a group; this may have to be put aside if a single black perpetrator is in danger of a custodial sentence if group treatment is not offered.

MANAGEMENT AND PRACTICE

Multi-agency working

Historically, treatment programmes in Britain have developed sporadically, as a result of the interest and initiative of a single probation officer or psychologists working in forensic services. As such their existence has been fragile, and utterly dependent upon the sustained commitment of the individuals involved. A multi-agency infrastructure at the local level is essential if treatment is to be integrated into a localised package of assessment, risk management, and child protection.

The Challenge Project—although originating from discussions between individual probation officers and a forensic clinical psychologist—emphasised the need for a multi-agency steering group, comprising managers in social services, the assistant chief probation officer and specialist senior probation officers, consultant child psychiatrists, and the author (forensic mental health). The inter-agency agreement drawn up by the steering group offered a means of consolidating ownership at a senior management level, explicitly stating the agency commitments and responsibilities, and providing simple practice guidance such as an anti-discriminatory policy and an interview procedure for potential therapists. Clinical supervision was provided by a subgroup of the steering group—all experienced practitioners—although of course each therapist retained professional accountability within their discipline and service. Joint supervisors from differing disciplines and agencies bring a richness to supervision which is lost within a single agency, but this relies upon a healthy working relationship between supervisors devoid of destructive envy. The complexity of the supervisory role may include monitoring the content of therapy and risk concerns, supporting therapists' personal feelings in relation to the work, developing the co-therapist relationship, highlighting group processes, and/or providing an informal teaching forum to enhance therapists' understanding of the perpetrators, their individual and group dynamics.

From a psychological perspective, a functional multi-agency structure avoids the polarisation of services into "advocates" for the victims and for the perpetrators, with all the secrecy, hostility, and shifting of responsibility that accompanies such a divide, and which so compellingly replicates the abusive situation. Providing a healthy, communicating "family" of agencies, who are able to exercise appropriate boundaries and allocate appropriate responsibility for the tasks of risk assessment, treatment, and child protection, is an important model for the perpetrator. Treatment providers can avoid being perceived as either colluding with the perpetrator or as holding the unique solution to future child protection concerns.

There are, of course, difficulties with multi-agency working, not least of which is negotiating the limits of confidentiality. It is probably impossible to lay out guidelines for every eventuality, and therapists, supervisors and the management group will need to be constantly reviewing and revising their practice. However it is important to tease out from the very beginning differences in approach. Whilst few practitioners or agencies would hesitate to agree that ongoing sexual abuse of a child requires immediate action, outside the therapeutic setting, there may be different approaches to new information about abuse in the past which emerges in assessment or treatment; agencies are likely to feel differently about this, dependent on whether the abuse occurred during a period of statutory supervision, how long ago it happened, whether it substantially alters the practitioners' view of the client and the risk he poses; some agencies may have a blanket rule that all new disclosures must be investigated regardless of the circumstances.

Philosophy

Practitioners with diverse backgrounds may have subtly or grossly divergent beliefs regarding the nature of child sexual abuse, and there is a risk that the complexity and pressure of treating perpetrators will highlight differences and allow for destructive splits to occur. An explicit programme philosophy can state common premises and common goals. Salter (1988) suggests a philosophy, which is quoted fully here:

1. Child molestation is either the result of:
   a) a deviant arousal pattern and/or
   b) the inappropriate conversion of nonsexual problems into sexual behaviour.
2. Goals of therapy for offenders are as follows:
   a) A primary goal is for offenders to learn to control their deviant arousal patterns.
   b) A second goal is to place obstacles in the path of converting nonsexual problems into sexual behaviour. These may include removing the father from the home, developing a better mother–child relationship, and improving the ability of the victim to be assertive and to report any attempts at remolestation. A key to minimising the risk of reoccurrence is to strengthen the positive qualities of the mother–child relationship.
   c) A third goal of therapy is for offenders and their families to learn to solve nonsexual problems in nonsexual ways. For example, the offenders need to deal with marital problems, depression, and other life problems directly, without the use of inappropriate sexual acting out.
3. Offenders must take responsibility for child sexual abuse without minimising, externalising, or projecting blame onto others. Manipulation and denial are major behavioural overlays of the offence and the response to discovery.
4. Each parent must take responsibility for his or her own behaviour and not the other's. Spouses are responsible for abuse only if they are involved in sexual abuse. They are responsible for denying and minimising if they do so.
5. Child sexual abuse is a treatable problem. Treatable is defined as helping the offender learn ways of minimising the risk of reoffence, it does not imply cure.

6. Any dysfunctional family patterns resulting from or providing the opportunity for sexual abuse need to be addressed and changed. These may include but are not restricted to isolation, poor communication, lack of boundaries, and patriarchal entitlement.
7. Victims are not responsible for child sexual abuse under any circumstances.
8. Child sexual abuse is harmful to children.
9. An important goal of a child sexual abuse programme is to provide support to other professionals and to network effectively.

Therapists

Any code of practice should contain reference to the balance of therapists (for example, gender, experience, or agency) and how they will be appointed, perhaps more implicitly, paying attention to the skills and personal qualities of potential therapists. It cannot be emphasised too strongly that the success of a programme may be as much due to the quality of the therapists and the supervisors, as to the content (Beckett et al., 1994). There is always a risk—particularly in structured treatment based on a philosophy of confronting denial—that therapy will become a substitute for retribution, a persecutory medium which justifies the expression of therapist hostility. Those working with perpetrators of child sexual abuse need to question whether they feel compassion for their clients, over and above abhorrence for the offending behaviour. There is often a fear that compassion or empathy will be confused with collusion, and that the practitioner may become contaminated with the perverse or distorted aspects of the perpetrator.

The therapist may experience difficulty in handling emotional intensity in the client group, or prefer to avoid the specifics of the abusive behaviour; he or she may need to be liked by their clients and avoid confronting dysfunctional attitudes; perhaps most important is the capacity to cope with therapeutic failure or ambiguity, as there are risks of false optimism and crushing discouragement in working with this client group. It is only by regular supervision that therapists can be helped to monitor their feelings towards the clients and to maintain the boundaries of the therapist–client relationship.

Ideally, therapists should be selected from a multi-agency interview, however informal. This allows for a more objective review of the individual's qualities, raises the profile of the role, and allows an escape route for not appointing unsuitable candidates. Where selection is not really feasible, it may be helpful to bring in outside consultation/supervision to exert a healthy influence over time. There often appears to be an over-concern with therapist gender mix, when it is probable that skills are more important in establishing effective treatment. Furthermore, consideration needs to be given to the therapist role in terms of balancing the needs of the service providers and the needs of the client group: consistent therapists (two or three) over a long period of time may be resource intensive but provide continuity and stability for the clients, whilst rotating therapists may spread the workload across agencies or personnel but have a markedly negative impact on the cohesion of a group or therapist–client alliance.

CLINICAL DECISIONS

There are a range of clinical questions confronting the practitioner, most of which do not have definitive answers, and many of which are influenced by service constraints. Some of the main dilemmas are outlined and will hopefully provide a starting point for discussion.

Are sex offender treatment programmes "therapy"?

There are a number of factors which differentiate the treatment of the perpetrator of child sexual abuse from other clients (or even other offenders). There is an acceptance of coerced participation in treatment, the offer of confidentiality is substantially reduced or non-existent, the perpetrator's behaviour is monitored outside of the treatment sessions, the helper role is rarely seen as being in conflict with the supervisory role, perpetrator anxieties may be used to facilitate disclosure rather than the emphasis on placing at ease, and the roles of adversary and ally are finely balanced in the practitioner (Ross, 1990). Furthermore, therapists are encouraged to make their value stance explicit, as proposed by Salter (1988): "The client should hear that the therapist does not believe that child sexual abuse is acceptable, that she has no intention of colluding with it in any way, that she believes that children are indeed reliable reporters of child sexual abuse whereas offenders are not reliable reporters of child sexual abuse, and that child sexual abuse is harmful to children. The offender should be further assured that the therapist considers it her job to prevent the re-occurrence of child sexual abuse in any form" (pp. 88–89).

Many of these factors raise serious questions about "therapy", but much will depend upon the capacity of the therapist to develop an empathic rapport with the offender. There is, for example, a world of difference between saying (or strongly implying) that the perpetrator is a liar, and openly acknowledging that there will be disagreement about certain issues. This has been discussed in greater depth in Chapter four. Nevertheless, services need to pay attention to the very real tensions between supervisory and treatment roles. The Challenge Project made a conscious decision to split these roles: the group leaders do not hold the probation orders or licences, and all serious concerns of risk are communicated to the field officer for them to act upon or not (social worker or health professional as appropriate); furthermore, additional reports to the criminal or civil courts are provided by the forensic mental health service and not the therapists when questions of risk and child protection are being considered. The perpetrator must be reassured about what will and will not be conveyed to other team members and agencies, if trust and rapport at any level are to be established.

The question of whether mandated treatment can be successful can only be answered by the fact that most sex offenders are initially coerced into programmes by fear of the alternatives—custody, no reunion with their family, or perhaps a wish for early custodial release. Unfortunately a superficial or externally driven motivation often dies away once the aversive consequences recede into the distance. Given that child sexual abuse is an assaultative behaviour which harms children, legal intervention and mandated therapy does seem justified. As Salter (1988) points out, otherwise the programme is counting on the offender's willingness to control his behaviour, which he has already explicitly demonstrated he is unable to do. The experience of the Challenge Project is that many apparently motivated perpetrators will continue to attend the programme after their statutory obligations have ceased until they face a deterioration in their personal circumstances, which brings feelings of rejection and resentment to the surface. However, we have also successfully engaged a number of voluntary perpetrators, despite the insistence on 100% attendance. The situation, however, might be viewed in a different light if a psychoanalytic psychotherapy were being considered; here, internally driven motivation is central to considering suitability for therapy. In such cases, court mandated treatment would contaminate the therapeutic process—particularly transference issues—and hinder progress.

Are some perpetrators unsuitable for community treatment?

The answer to this is probably very few, putting to one side the criminal justice system requirements for retribution and deterrence. Impulsivity and compliance are the two issues to consider: if a perpetrator has demonstrated high levels of impulsivity in the past, to the extent that he appears to have very limited capacity to resist compelling urges to assault children, then he should perhaps only enter a community treatment programme if he is willing to take anti-libidinal medication. It must be noted that such medication has a range of unpleasant side-effects and, medico-legally, can never be included in a mandated treatment programme. Such perpetrators are rare, and a more difficult consideration is compliance: generally speaking, a substantial history of various antisocial behaviours, chronic social instability, and/or significant drug and alcohol misuse—before as well as during the period of offending behaviour—will be poor prognostic signs. The Challenge Project (Craissati & McClurg, 1997) found that a history of childhood sexual victimisation *and* a previous history of sexual or violent offending, together were highly predictive of non-compliance in the treatment programme (see Chapter seven). This should act as a warning to practitioners who are likely to empathise with the abused, chaotic, and vulnerable perpetrator, that in fact such a history may raise obstacles to engagement in treatment.

Who is suitable for treatment?

It is perhaps easiest to start with a discussion of who might not be suitable for treatment, as these will form a smaller group of perpetrators.

Total denial.   The perpetrator must accept at least some responsibility for the abuse and thus agree that his behaviour may have been problematic. Total deniers are probably best challenged within the prison system—not least because a recommendation for community treatment becomes unviable—when some may shift their attitude over time.

Serious mental illness.   A history of psychosis—often in the form of hallucinations or delusions—must be taken seriously as it automatically indicates the fragility of the perpetrator's internal world. Such individuals are prone to break down under stress and may experience their therapist in a very real sense as a persecutor. Both confrontational group therapy and intensive exploratory therapy may shake the perpetrator's sense of self in relation to the outside world and precipitate psychosis or suicide. This is not to say that mentally ill sex offenders cannot engage in psychological treatment, but it must be embarked upon cautiously, with the close involvement of a psychiatrist.

Psychological disturbance.   This refers to those symptoms of psychological disturbance which may interfere with offence-related treatment. A history of repetitive self-harming behaviour where the perpetrator is at best ambivalent about discussing the offending, is likely to re-occur during treatment, and divert the therapist from the offending. Similarly, a strong propensity to somatise (to express emotional turbulence in terms of physical symptoms) will result in frequent absences with accompanying sick notes. This is particularly problematic with elderly perpetrators who are unlikely to be dealt with harshly by the courts should they fail to attend treatment. In both cases, it may be worth considering supportive therapy or close monitoring only, as an alternative to custody or intensive treatment.

Brain damage.   Perpetrators with specific and significant brain damage should be managed by the relevant mental health service, as impulsivity and sexual disinhibition will probably require additional treatments. However perpetrators with a learning disability or mild level of impairment can usually participate in mainstream treatment if their communication and cognitive skills allow them to keep pace with others. The difficulty with someone who presents as "simple" in a group is that the other group members do not take their behaviour seriously, and collude with the individual's own wish to hide behind his intellectual disability.

Primary substance misuse. A few perpetrators will present with a long-standing alcohol dependency problem, and even fewer with a significant drug problem. In these instances, it is imperative that treatment is initially sought for the substance misuse problem; once stabilised, sex offender treatment can begin. However for the vast majority of perpetrators, heavy drinking at the time of the offence would not preclude them from entering a sex offender programme immediately, and perhaps attending a community alcohol project concurrently.

Dangerousness. There are a few perpetrators whose offence history has escalated to such a degree, or contains evidence of sadism which indicates that they undoubtedly pose a high threat of very severe physical harm to children in the community. It is questionable whether such individuals should ever receive mandated treatment upon their release into the community, or even voluntarily join a group treatment programme, given the poor prognosis. The impact of renewed offending would be to jeopardise the programme or clinic through loss of public and institutional confidence. Such perpetrators occasional present to services desperately seeking help, and should be offered individual support by a highly experienced practitioner or multidisciplinary team.

Are there times when psycho-analytically orientated psychotherapy is the treatment of choice?

There is no doubt that the body of research evidence supports the use of cognitive–behavioural approaches (see Chapter seven) in treating perpetrators of child sexual abuse. Nevertheless, psychoanalysts have presented single case studies on apparently successful treatments of incest perpetrators, although there is considerably more pessimism about fixated paedophiles. The Portman Clinic in London places a number of sexually deviant individuals in long-term group psychotherapy with reported benefits.

More often than not, the criteria for suitability for psychoanalytic psychotherapy are not met by perpetrators of child sexual abuse, often quite simply because of their levels of denial. Coltart (1987) refers to nine factors necessary in the patient: a capacity to take a distance from his own emotional experience; self-reflection as a result of being listened to; quality of affect; a capacity to perceive relationships between history and current discomfort; a capacity to recognise and tolerate internal reality; a lively curiosity and concern about this internal reality; some capacity for the use of the imagination; a capacity to recognise the existence of an unconscious mental life; signs of success in some limited area of life, and proper self-esteem in relation to this.

Suitably "psychologically-minded" perpetrators may benefit from a more psychodynamic approach when they present with little denial or few distortions in relation to their offending behaviour, as much of the impact of a cognitive–

behavioural programme will be lost. For some of these perpetrators, their own histories of childhood deprivation and sexual victimisation might pose the most difficult area of emotional conflict, glossed over and avoided where possible in treatment. Of course it is important to distinguish between genuine accept-ance and superficial compliance (often acquired by participation in a previous programme).

Is group treatment preferable to individual treatment?

Estella Welldon (unpublished, Foulkes Lecture, 1996), in discussing the use of group therapy for socially and sexually deviant patients, suggests that group therapy offers patients the benefit of being able to interact with the social micro-cosm of group therapy which can afford them a much better understanding of their problems since they are so deeply related to antisocial actions. She sug-gests that patients who have experienced their relationship with one parent as intense and suffocating find groups provide them with a much warmer and less threatening atmosphere than they could find in individual therapy in which their experience of authority is so intense. In contrast, the patient who has never experi-enced satisfactory relationships in early life (those from very large families with financial deprivation and emotional overcrowding) is likely to respond better to individual treatment. Issues relating to adoption, fostering and placement in care as a child will all re-emerge in the group situation, as the patient struggles to "fit in".

Groups provide the collective aspect which offers an alternative experience to the isolation, secretiveness, and shame central to child sexual abuse. Perpetrators discover that they are not alone, and in doing so provide each other with support, recognition of each others' perspectives and distortions, feedback and model-ling. Confrontation by peers, when the perpetrators are involuntary, is far more effective than the potential therapist–patient battle. What the perpetrator loses in terms of individual attention, he gains in terms of generalised learning from other group members' experiences in the group.

Individual therapy may be the treatment of choice for perpetrators with fragile mental states (see above), prominent voyeuristic tendencies, or chaotically perverse presentations (where sexual offending targets a range of victims and a number of deviant behaviours are engaged in). The fixated paedophile longing to talk about his fantasy and offending history, and aroused in doing so, will cause trouble in a group where he insists that other group members are not being as "honest" in their disclosures as himself. It is a difficult task for the therapists to establish treatment as therapy not pornography in such cases. The alternative —individual treatment—may be overwhelming for the therapist who is likely to be drawn into a sado-masochistic relationship with such a perpetrator and emerge from sessions feeling assaulted themselves or overwhelmingly angry.

The research does not clearly distinguish between outcomes of group and individual treatment. The Challenge Project (Craissati & McClurg, 1997) found that there was a greater trend towards improved outcome in the group treatment subjects than in individual treatment subjects, when both received identical offence-focused programmes (see Chapter seven). Group treatment should theoretically be more resource-efficient, but in practice, considerably more time and effort is generally put into group work in terms of planning, recruitment, feedback, and supervision. It is perhaps unfortunate that the efforts of individual practitioners are being undermined by the focus on groups; this is reflected in the court's (and other agencies') preference that treatment is provided as a group programme, thus taking little account of the treatment which many skilled and experienced practitioners are providing in the course of fulfilling their professional role.

What format should the group treatment take?

Therapists. Welldon (unpublished, Foulkes Lecture, 1996) advocates the use of one therapist only in group analytic therapy, in order to avoid the re-creation of "the primal scene in its most concrete terms, which is potential dynamite for our patients". Most practitioners would tend towards two co-therapists for group work, preferably balanced male and female. It is not clear how far the gender mix matters: most patients will be sensitive to differential therapist confidence, skill and style, and will relate to them accordingly. The dangers of re-creating the primary relationships are to foster idealisation and inevitable denigration in the perpetrators, envious impulses are barely contained, and any opportunity is seized to redress earlier humiliations and triumphantly break up "parental bonding". The therapists need to maintain a solid working relationship which is constantly on guard for attacks to the integrity of their relationship. Interestingly, the Challenge Project had two female therapists for some time, and this appeared to be instrumental in promoting a significant improvement in attitudes towards women, as measured on standardised questionnaires (Craissati & McClurg, 1997). Some agencies choose to co-work clients outside of a group programme, and this may be an important means of developing the skills of inexperienced officers, and managing the demands and anxieties raised by this client group. However there is a danger in co-working (strength in numbers) being inadvertently used to break down denial or control a difficult perpetrator which may result in angry retaliation or false acquiescence.

Frequency of therapy. Currently, group treatment programmes are run either weekly, in short intensive blocks, or a combination of both. There seem to be advantages and disadvantages to both: weekly therapy allows for change to occur slowly and to be assimilated into everyday life; feedback can offer clues to improvements in coping strategies; however there is a danger that the work of the session can be lost all too easily during the week. Intensive blocks carry a momentum with them which allows for a sharp learning curve; what is unclear is whether this learning is internalised, and there is no opportunity for feedback and monitoring. The number of hours of treatment vary greatly between programmes, but are likely to fall between 50–100 hours. However, this is unlikely to be sufficient for a high deviancy group where change is very slow (Beckett et al., 1994).

Slow open or closed group.   Whilst a closed group provides stability for perpetrators and therapists alike, and allows for the possibility of intensive blocks of treatment, there are some striking disadvantages: firstly, the courts and parole board are concerned about delays in commencing treatment of more than a few weeks; this could be dealt with by bridging the gap with irregular brief sessions to discuss the group and keep the offences alive in the perpetrator's mind; secondly, a closed group loses the opportunity for "senior" members to confront "junior" members therapeutically; such evidence of growing understanding and emotional development enhances the perpetrator's feelings of self-worth in a way which was never available in childhood.

Membership.   The Challenge Project commenced with a policy of child sexual abusers only for two simple reasons: there were a large number on our caseload, and we felt more confident in treating them. It is likely that many of the programmes around the country mirrored this thinking, despite compelling evidence from the United States (Ryan et al., 1987) that mixed child molester/rapist groups provided creative material for confrontation. It is generally true that perpetrators against adult women present as more treatment resistant and are more likely to reoffend sexually or violently (Thornton & Travers, 1991). Excluding the most overtly violent or sadistic perpetrators against adults will both create a more containing therapeutic environment, but also stop child abusers hiding behind the "I'm not a rapist" camouflage. Nevertheless, six fixated paedophiles in a group is a ring, not therapy. It is essential to include as broad a range of perpetrators as possible—that is, aim for modified homogeneity—who will develop a greater understanding of all the dynamic and cognitive processes involved.

THE CASE STUDIES

Tom was considered appropriate for group treatment (cognitive–behavioural) because this would provide the opportunity to develop warm and supportive relationships with the other group members, in contrast to his confrontational macho style in the outside world. The intensity of his relationship with his profoundly abusive father mitigated against individual treatment, where the transference was likely to be overwhelming in terms of his fear of dependency and need to rebel against threatening intimacy. Relatively low levels of denial meant that he could help other group members face up to their own distortions, whilst he would find other aspects of the programme emotionally challenging.

Peter was placed in the group (cognitive–behavioural) essentially because the court wished it, and we were concerned to try treatment as an alternative to a very brief custodial sentence. The high levels of sexual deviancy and antisocial behaviour in the past posed a problem to both group or individual work. It was felt that the group might be able to contain some of the perverse dynamics which would erupt in individual work in terms of a battle for control. The therapists anticipated a battle of sorts regarding boundaries—time keeping, completing homework, and alcohol.

George was placed in individual therapy, with a focus on psychodynamic processes linking his own early sexual victimisation with his unconscious motives for offending. His very low levels of denial rendered the cognitive–behavioural approach largely redundant, and the utter deprivation he suffered in childhood suggested that he needed the experience of a consistent, boundaried and attentive therapist on whom he could develop a healthy level of dependency.

Kevin was considered to be ideally suited to the cognitive–behavioural group approach because of the nature of his denial. His distorted perceptions were readily apparent but not overly fixed, many of them were held on to in an attempt to preserve some self-esteem. It was felt that he might accept challenges from his peers more readily than from a potential individual female therapist who could provoke much of his ambivalent feelings towards his mother.

CHAPTER SIX

Treatment content

The majority of group treatment programmes in Britain today follow much the same format, with greater or lesser emphasis on some aspects of therapy. For example, there will be differences between programmes where the philosophy leans towards the sexual addiction model (Salter, 1988) in contrast to services which traditionally have placed sex offender treatment in the context of aversive life experiences and emotional trauma. Helpful overviews of multi-factorial/cognitive–behavioural treatment programmes can be found in Salter (1988) and Morrison, Erooga, and Beckett (1994); and Maletzky (1991) provides a comprehensive approach to behavioural treatments. This chapter aims to provide the reader with a detailed account of a group cognitive–behavioural approach—the favoured method of treatment currently.

PROGRAMME COMPONENTS

There are approximately seven main components to most treatment programmes, as detailed in Beckett et al. (1994):

1. Denial and minimisation are targeted, as breaking down denial is viewed as an important prerequisite for change and the assumption of responsibility.
2. Victim empathy is developed by educating perpetrators as to the harmful effect of abuse, the aim being to strengthen the motivation not to offend.
3. Justifications and cognitive distortions are elicited and challenged so as to stop the pattern of assuaging feelings of guilt and giving oneself permission to offend.

4. Lifestyle and personality addresses the issues of low self-esteem, fear of adult intimacy and inappropriate assertiveness, so often found in perpetrators, with the aim of improving functioning in society.
5. Deviant sexual fantasies are one predictor of reoffending and are therefore targeted in order to help the perpetrator modify or control deviant arousal, and develop acceptable fantasies as an alternative.
6. Relapse prevention aims to help perpetrators recognise risky situations, feelings, moods and thoughts, and to develop strategies to prevent relapse.

Some of these components are addressed as separate topics, whilst others are best incorporated into the general content.

METHODS IN GROUP TREATMENT

This type of structured format usually includes the following techniques.

Discussion. Discussion takes place on a theme or around an exercise; it offers an opportunity to assess the quantity and quality of a group member's contributions and interactions, and particular characteristics such as domination, scapegoating or withdrawal in the group may be observed.

"Hot seat". The "hot seat" is a favoured technique where a group member sits centre stage and undertakes a piece of work—usually directly offence-focused—which is commented upon by the therapists and other group members; it must be carefully handled in order not to be persecutory for the "victim", thereby reinforcing denial, or voyeuristic for the others; nevertheless it offers an opportunity to observe group members' ability to constructively challenge each other and demonstrate their own learning.

Victim or perpetrator material (written or video). Such material provides a more articulate account of sexual abuse and its impact, than either the perpetrator or his victim may be willing or able to communicate; it can be very moving, yet non-threatening to the extent that the perpetrator is not confronted by his own victim.

Role play. Role play may or may not include the therapists and can be instrumental in provoking powerful thoughts or feelings, to be commented upon; some role plays (such as debates) may be intellectual exercises, whilst role playing victims may bring emotions to the fore.

Small group exercises. Breaking into small groups has a number of functions: it may force unconfident or withdrawn group members to work more productively; it develops rapport between group members who may have to disclose personal material; it allows the therapists to assess empathic skills, particularly if each member has to report back his partner's experiences or views. However it is important to pay attention to the groupings, sometimes pairing "senior" with "junior" members, and at other times, matching pairs of equal "standard".

Homework.   Homework is usually required between some or all of the sessions; it may take the form of a weekly diary, or occasional exercises, and will encourage group members to think about the group content during the week; it is often an area where non-compliance may represent the group member's ambivalence towards treatment, or underlying self-consciousness about poor literacy skills.

SEQUENCE OF TREATMENT

Salter (1988) suggests that techniques which are the most effective in controlling the behaviour in the short run should be introduced first to reduce the chance of reoffending. This usually includes behavioural approaches to altering deviant arousal patterns. If deviant fantasies are not addressed early on in treatment, the perpetrator may be much less willing to re-open the subject later. Beckett (1994) suggests that homework exercises should be introduced early on, so that the expectations of treatment are clear and any resistance can be addressed. Once the desire to reoffend is under control, cognitive distortions, victim empathy, and interpersonal skill training can be addressed.

It is essential to commence therapy with a full account of the offending behaviour, as this sets the agenda for treatment which is offence-focused and without "secrets". Most perpetrators fear this aspect of the group programme and will not be able to participate fully or concentrate until "the worst is over".

THE BOUNDARIES OF TREATMENT

Before group treatment can be embarked upon, the boundaries must be clearly set. This is important both for the group members, some of whom are likely to break or bend the rules, and for the therapists who must be clear and consistent in decision-making. Furthermore, the criminal justice system will be concerned to know that treatment requirements are rigorous and strictly adhered to, if the programme is to retain its respect. Unclear limit-setting allows for unhealthy dynamics to encroach on treatment, and directly replicates the offending situation where fundamental adult/child boundaries have been violated: the therapists may feel themselves too paralysed to act, or alternatively slip into a punitive set of responses. Clearly not every eventuality can be planned for, but common issues such as late attendance, missed sessions, alcohol consumption, and non-completion of homework tasks can be clearly laid out in the programme policy or contract.

The Challenge Project group programme decided to set out the following responses to some boundary issues:

1. Alcohol use: expelled from session.
2. Late attendance: after 10 minutes, not allowed in.
3. Non-completion of homework: must be completed, referrer can help or module repeated.
4. Missed sessions: medical sick note required, 2+ sessions sick, redo module.

Warnings are initially given verbally, and subsequently in writing with a copy to the referrer (usually probation officer or social worker). A further incident results in discharge from the group which, if treatment is mandated, is likely to result in breach or recall procedings.

RECORDING, REVIEWING AND COMMUNICATING

It is probably advisable that a recording sheet is developed, and completed for each group member after every session. The purpose of this is broadly twofold: to monitor a group member's progress over time, and to maintain a formal record of treatment in case of renewed concerns of offending, judicial proceedings, or if warnings and possibly discharge become necessary.

A recording sheet should be as concise as possible, including headings such as attendance, participation, content, concerns. In the Challenge Project, these recording sheets are treated primarily as internal documents. There is a Module Report (see Fig. 6.1), completed at the end of each module, which documents more generally performance, progress and areas highlighted for attention. These will be given to the group member himself, who is allowed to add his comments, and copies sent to the referrer and, where appropriate, social services child protection proceedings.

Many treatment programmes include more intrusive styles of recording and observation, such as videotaping, and live supervision by means of two-way mirrors and telephone links. There is no doubt that direct observation provides the most vivid learning tool for the therapists and an opportunity for the managers of the service to check the quality of the programme. However, there are a number of powerful contraindications to intrusive observation: the voyeuristic nature of two-way mirrors may feed the perpetrator's own voyeuristic tendencies, and provide, in a very concrete way, a target for longstanding paranoid or persecutory fears in group members; it may have the unfortunate consequence of exacerbating therapist anxieties and locating the "expertise"—in their eyes and the group members' eyes—on the other side of the mirror.

The group member's attendance and participation, despite being addressed regularly in supervision, should be formally reviewed at intervals during treatment.

Challenge Project Modular Report

Name: **Date:**

Module:

Absences (no. & reasons):

Circulation list:

Participation (eg, punctuality, homework tasks, spontaneous contributions):

Comments (eg, specific content, areas requiring further work, child protection / mental health concerns):

Group member's response:

Signed (therapist):   **Date:**

Signed (client):   **Date:**

FIG. 6.1   Example of module report.

It may be, if someone's participation is unsatisfactory, that explicit goals can be set for the next few weeks, and again reviewed. The therapists may wish to agree between themselves to focus on certain areas of weakness in a group member's functioning, and so on.

Close communication with relevant services is an important component in managing perpetrators and maintaining healthy working relationships with other agencies. Probation officers with statutory responsibilities can easily feel excluded from treatment; social services may have unrealistic expectations of the treatment outcome, or could be providing an essential adjunct to treatment by engaging the spouse in supportive child protection work. However, liaison must always be open and the limits of confidentiality repeatedly clarified so that the perpetrator can feel able to contribute without fearing that every comment will be relayed on: once communicated, information passes beyond any control of the therapists.

PROCESS ISSUES

Content deals with the group subject matter, tasks, and explicit focus of the group; process relates to the underlying group and individual dynamics and inter-actions. These processes may be relatively easily accessed and understood, when hostility, collusion, competitiveness and seductiveness are operating just below the surface of a group. Other dynamics originate deep in the unconscious, often emerging in a group as a replication of the early family relationships with all the disturbance so often experienced by perpetrators of child sexual abuse. Attention to process issues will deepen rapport with the group, and will provide an opportunity for group members to explore personal and interpersonal dynamics; it becomes an urgent matter when process threatens to undermine the stability of the group, or to sabotage progress. The therapists will undoubtedly struggle to maintain a balance between content and process, and this will be a recurrent theme in supervision.

The Challenge Project—despite the programme content reflecting a cognitive–behavioural approach—draws heavily on psychoanalytic thinking as a model for understanding process (see Chapter two for an outline of the psychoanalytic model). Many psychoanalytic terms are reasonably familiar to practitioners who may feel more or less comfortable in using the concepts: splitting, projecting, identifying with the aggressor, and transference are perhaps the most widely re-cognised. Since an understanding of these concepts offer a means of recognising and managing problems in the therapeutic process, it is worth outlining them in some detail.

Splitting and projecting

Splitting and projection are both described as primitive defence mechanisms, which is to say early manoeuvres developed by the infant to deal with the anxiety of his utter dependency and own destructive feelings. Splitting acts to

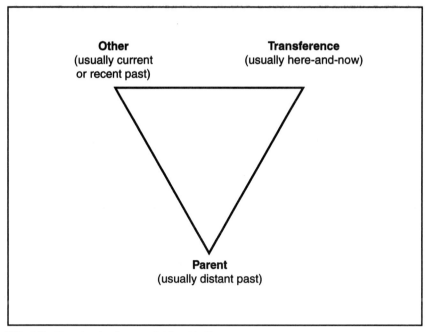

FIG. 6.2   The triangle of person (Malan, 1979).

keep apart frightening contradictory feelings, images or aspects of an object, because of the individual's difficulty in tolerating such ambivalence or ambiguity. For example the "madonna–whore" split is often encountered in extreme forms in sex offenders, who perhaps idealise their mothers or partners, but express their rage and feelings of impotence in relation to their victims who have been defiled and humiliated. Projection refers to unwanted or destructive parts of the self which are split off and projected into objects (or others) where they reside temporarily, unavailable to the self (Steiner, 1993). Commonly sex offenders will identify hostility and destructiveness in others (the courts, the child's new step-father, other more overtly violent offenders) which is in fact their own anger, split off and located elsewhere. This is particularly evident in the fixated paedophile who may cling to an idealised portrayal of his relationship with the child, unable to tolerate the realisation of his own destructive impulses.

Transference and countertransference

Transference can be defined simply as the patient's feelings from the past (or even any feelings) which are then transferred to the therapist or the therapeutic situation (Malan, 1979). Malan explains the mechanism by means of a triangle, the triangle of person (see Fig. 6.2): the aim of psychodynamic therapy being to make links between the three points of the triangle, using transference interpretations to trace feelings towards the therapist and/or others in the patient's life back to their origin in the past. In structured group treatment, it is important to understand these links, although therapists will need to decide how best to manage the key transference issues.

> An example of transference interfering with the group content occurred with **Kevin**, at a time when there was a female and male co-therapist team: he had formed an alliance with the female therapist, who in turn had been able to draw him out on a number of important topics; nevertheless, it was the female therapist who placed him under some pressure for having failed to complete his sexual fantasy diary homework; he became increasingly entrenched in denying any sexual fantasies, and withdrew from participating in the group, although he was not able to express any anger directly. It seemed possible to understand this behaviour in terms of transference issues: Kevin felt betrayed by the female therapist who he experienced as having shifted from a nurturing to a sexually intrusive position, which replicated feelings related to his ex-partner who he felt should have been dependent upon him, but instead humiliated him under the influence of her "witch" of a mother; although not easily accessible to him consciously, it could be hypothesised that these were feelings originating in Kevin's relationship with his mother where mutual dependency alternated with sexual humiliation and rejection.

Countertransference, as defined by Heimann (1950) covers all the feelings which the therapist experiences towards the patient, many of which will offer a source of insight into the patient's unconscious conflicts and defences. Some of these issues have been discussed briefly in Chapter five in relation to therapist attributes and feelings. One of the central strengths of supervision and/or personal therapy is to enable the therapist to sustain the feelings stirred up and to subordinate them to the therapeutic task in which she functions as the patient's mirror reflection (Heimann, 1950). Occasionally therapists cannot stop themselves from acting on their feelings, resulting in overly punitive or passive responses, broken boundaries, envious conflict with co-therapists, and so on.

> **Peter** caused havoc with the group initially until the therapists were able to deal with their feelings in supervision and to devise ways of managing him which did not result in destructive and escalating confrontations. They interpreted his need to keep themselves and the group members at a distance by using sexually explicit details to assault others, and suggested this was an attempt to avoid the pain of looking at the feelings which lay beneath his offending. They subsequently adopted a rather behavioural approach whereby he received no response or encouragement if talking about sex, but received considerable positive feedback on discussion of other issues. Although there was no suggestion that this approach had any impact on his fixated interest, it did have an enormous impact on the quality of his membership of the group, and his capacity (at an intellectual level) to listen to the therapeutic material.

Identification with the aggressor

Identification with the aggressor was first outlined by Anna Freud (1936) and exemplified in Alice Miller's accounts of the uses of splitting, denial and idealisation in individuals who are treated harshly as children (Miller, 1987): in order to survive the trauma of being victimised, the "patient" has to split off and deny the persecutory aspects of the object (abuser), thereby preserving a positive and idealised image; in later life, when perhaps these split-off part objects are reactivated, the "patient" now identifies with the idealised aggressor, and acts accordingly, defending against the memory of his original traumas and his vulnerable sense of self.

> This psychological mechanism can be seen to be operating quite clearly in **George** whose need to believe that his abusers cared for him led to a denial of the destructive aspects of the relationship—all of which re-emerged in his abuse of John. In the group setting, it was **Tom** who unconsciously re-enacted his father's role, taunting the others with suggestions of what he might reveal, leaving them feeling brutalised by his accounts of physical and emotional victimisation, yet failing to relate to group members as separate individuals in their own right.

THE CHALLENGE PROJECT TREATMENT PROGRAMME

The Challenge Project provides individual and group treatment. The core group programme lasts one year, meeting on a weekly basis for one and a half hours (subsequently extended to two hours). Membership can range from 6–8 men, all of whom have committed offences against children. The group composition reflects the agencies' caseload at that time, and usually has a preponderance of intra-familial offenders, one or two fixated perpetrators and one or two moderately violent or antisocial perpetrators (again more recently the structure has expanded to include recidivist indecent exposers and sexual offenders against adults where no excessive violence was used). The group runs a slow, open structure, and new members can be admitted at the beginning of a module, which usually entails a maximum wait of four weeks. Two week breaks are planned for summer, Christmas and Easter, as well as bank holidays. At any one time, there are three therapists involved in a group—two probation officers with specialist training, and a psychologist. Two therapists run the group, whilst the third monitors the video recording. This arrangement minimises disruption whilst allowing therapists to take holidays without anyone running the group alone.

The relapse prevention group runs separately, twice a year, and meets on a weekly basis for 10 weeks. It is run by a probation officer and a psychologist. Membership comprises men who have completed the core group, or who are on short periods of statutory supervision and have already completed an offending cycle; high risk offenders are prioritised.

TABLE 6.1
Challenge Project intensive treatment programme

No. of weeks	Module	Description
1 per member	1: offence disclosure	Detailed "hot seat" account of offending: thoughts, feelings, behaviours and antecedants
5	1: offence cycle	Development of individual cycles (Ryan et al., 1987)
6	3: victim empathy	Explorations of members' own childhood victimisations —general and sexual—highlighting short/long term impact, and experiences of revenge/retaliation
4	4: relationships	Parental bonding experiences, sexual discoveries and development, 'first love' and romance
4	4: relationships	Stereotypes about women, adult sexual experiences and relationships, tracing problems with intimacy back to early experiences
6	3: victim empathy	Power and informed consent, victim experiences, apology letters
4	2: offending cycle	Reviewing and adding to cycle, identifying weak spots, decision matrix
1 per member	1: offence disclosure	Excerpts of video of original disclosure, amend and review progress, including group members' feedback

The programme is cognitive–behavioural in concept, and largely derivative (influenced by work in the United States, Canada, and Britain). Its format is modular: four modules split into two parts each. Table 6.1 is an outline of the programme format. An explicit decision, based on the nature of the client group, was made not to provide components on comprehensive sex education, substance misuse, assertiveness training, general gender power issues, or detailed fantasy modification procedures. For those perpetrators who were assessed as having significant problems in one of the above areas, they were either referred on to the relevant services or the referrer was able to focus on the issue. Specifically, behavioural fantasy modification therapy and medication (for either mental health or anti-libidinal purposes) was available from the local multidisciplinary forensic mental health team. Although the assessment questionnaires are for research, not clinical, purposes, the treatment content was designed to incorporate many of the constructs contained within the Multiphasic Sex Inventory and the empathy scale.

There are essential language rules for the group: therapists are discouraged from using jargon at any time, but to explain concepts in clear and precise words; sexual and offence-related language must be explicit—"I abused my daughter" is not acceptable.

It was decided that supervision should take place on a weekly basis, shared between the probation and the forensic mental health service. Its focus is primarily client-based, but attention is given to strong feelings in the therapists. Essentially supervision is confidential, except at the point where a therapist's behaviour or emotional state threatened their professional integrity or fundamental coping skills.

No perpetrator is accepted for treatment unless witness statements—or at the very least a verbatim statement by a professional of the victim's allegation—are available. The therapists must be familiar with the content of the statements—particularly the names and ages of victims and exact convictions—and reread the file at frequent intervals throughout the treatment programme. There are two main reasons for this: firstly the perpetrators are quick to point out inaccuracies and thereby undermine the impact of a therapist's intervention; secondly, the victims rarely have a three-dimensional quality in the perpetrator's minds, and having been reduced to object status, are easily abused; it is for the therapists to emphasise the very real individuality of the victims and bring them alive in the group.

CONTRACT

Prior to commencing group treatment, each perpetrator is invited to meet with the therapists, and sign a contract detailing the Project's expectations of him. A sample contract reads as follows:

Challenge Project: Contract of Attendance

Agreement between group members and group leaders for attendance at the Challenge Project Group.

1. I agree to attend for a minimum of one year.
   I understand that my membership of the group will be reviewed every 10 weeks, and that the group leaders reserve the right to ask me to leave the group at any time.
2. I understand that if I miss any appointments, my probation officer/social worker/doctor will be notified.
   If I miss two consecutive appointments, action will be taken.
   If I miss appointments persistently this may lead to exclusion from the group.
3. I understand that I attend the Challenge Project group in addition to other supervision by probation officer/social worker/doctor.
4. I agree that feedback will be given to my supervisory officer/social worker/doctor regularly and that I will see all communications about me that are sent out.
5. I understand that if I disclose any offending behaviour since my conviction that this will be made known to my supervisory officer/social worker/doctor.
6. If I or the group leaders feel that either I or children are unsafe I understand that my social worker/supervisory officer/doctor will be informed.
7. Whilst any previous offences that I disclose will normally be kept confidential within the group, I understand that the group leaders reserve the right to act upon such information outside of the group.
   I promise not to disclose any information that I may hear to anyone outside of the group.

8. I understand that the Challenge Project is being evaluated and as part of the evaluation I shall be expected to complete questionnaires at the beginning and end of the treatment. Although the data will be evaluated, I understand that I shall remain anonymous.

9. I understand that group members are not encouraged to meet or socialise outside of the group and I agree that should any do this, I will undertake to bring this information to group sessions.

10. I understand that the group leaders will be supervised in their work and that this will involve disclosure of the content of these group meetings.

11. I understand that a video tape is made of group sessions for the purposes of treatment and supervision. I also understand that there will be times when extracts of the video will be wanted for training purposes.
I give my permission for the tape to be shown to professional people only, provided that all reference to a surname or other identifying words are deleted from the tape.

12. I understand that as a condition of my attendance at the Challenge Project I must register with a general practitioner and inform the group leaders of the name and address of my doctor.

13. I will inform the group leaders of any change of address.

14. I understand that I may be required to attend a Relapse Prevention group after my core group membership has ended. This will be discussed with me by my probation officer/group leader/other.

15. I agree not to consume alcohol or use drugs before attending the group.

Signed..........................Date.............................
Group member

Signed..........................Date.............................
Group leader

Offence disclosure

Aim.   To elicit a detailed account of the offending behaviour, and the events leading up to it, which encourages increasingly open disclosure and a gradual assumption of full responsibility.

Content.   By the start of treatment, the perpetrator will probably have given an account of his offending behaviour to a variety of professionals, but never to an audience of strange men in a personalised setting. The skill for the therapists is to maximise the information they can elicit whilst maintaining an empathic support atmosphere. Those members who will talk with superficial ease about their sexually abusive behaviour, should be encouraged to concentrate on the cycle of thoughts and feelings preceding their behaviour; members who hide behind feelings of shame must not be allowed to fudge their actions, as recorded by the witness statements, and discrepancies can be pointed out. Chapter four details the complexity of managing denial and is very pertinent to these sessions. Confrontational styles should be muted and much of the questioning should be exploratory rather than critical, bringing the perpetrator back to the subject when necessary. The account should be written on a flip-chart or video recorded, and transcribed for later use and revision. The session closes with some discussion of glaring distortions or justifications in the account.

The following is an extract of **Kevin**'s account in his first session of sexually abusing Sally. The main areas of interest are in bold:

> . . . "Sally asked for a cuddle one night and after the third time I got aroused. **I put a stop to it. She started to touch me and one thing led to another** . . . I didn't get her back to her room as soon as I should have . . . Nothing happened for two months. She sat in the place that was for whoever was in favour. **She was always tight up against me. On one occasion I told Sally it mustn't go on, I was held over a barrel by a 12-year-old, she knew what was going on was wrong, so did I. I swear to God I never woke her up for sex**, it was **addictive**, like the booze, but there was no way it was going to go any further . . ."

After the initial disclosure session, every group member has to introduce himself and his offending whenever a new member joins. In this way, the newcomer is given information and "senior" members are reminded of the reasons for their own presence in the group; this can promote a sense of equality, create openness, and allow for the monitoring of other members who should not be allowed to become complacent. They must refer to their convictions, sentence, a brief behavioural summary of the offending behaviour, the name, age and relationship to the victim, and their view on who is to blame.

Homework.   To write up an account of his offending behaviour.

Offence cycle

Aim.   To identify in detail the process by which the perpetrator moves to a high risk situation and then offends, and in doing so to continue to reduce denial and justifications.

Content.   The Project uses the sexual assault cycle developed by Lane and presented in Ryan et al. (1987). The model is presented to the group, and the headings explained. One group member is chosen as an example and the group encouraged to suggest material for the various headings. In a subsequent session, the group is split into pairs and encouraged to develop cycles with each other. Later the members feed back to the larger group, one by one, allowing for contributions from other group members and the leaders.

Group members will differ in the degree to which their cycle is loaded under certain headings; for example some will flounder after they have identified the early development of their own emotional difficulties, others will be clear about their fantasies and subsequent stages, struggling when it comes to understanding the non sexual motivation. Although members should be encouraged eventually to develop a balanced cycle, it should be borne in mind that some perpetrators, for example, probably do not experience deviant fantasies prior to offending. Others may experience powerful fantasies of revenge against another adult, or thoughts of being caught which accompany the sexual arousal involved in offending.

Below are two examples of offence cycles, Tom and Peter (Figs 6.3 and 6.4, respectively) where the difference between a sexually fixated and intrafamilial type of offender can be seen.

> **Tom** was generally very emotional in therapy and able to identify—although not resolve—the pattern of painful thoughts and feelings preceding his offending behaviour; his assaults on Mary were clearly accompanied by violent thoughts aimed at seeking pleasure through control and exercising revenge. **Peter**, on the other hand, clearly demonstrated the ease with which he expressed his sexual excitement, and had to be stopped from detailing his fantasy material; however, he was puzzled by the pressure placed on him to explore thoughts and feelings which may have underpinned his deviant sexual arousal, and his impoverished capacity for emotional understanding is evident in the cycle.

Homework.   To add to the offence cycle and present to the group.

Victim awareness—self as victim

Aim.   To develop both an intellectual understanding of the impact of victimisation on children, and an emotional insight into the experience, by means of exploring the perpetrator's own victim experience.

Content.   Practitioners are often ambivalent about dealing with the subject of perpetrators' own victimisation experiences—sexual or otherwise—because of the fear that they might collude with a denial of responsibility. Yet, much of the difficulty for perpetrators in contemplating a more empathic stance towards their victim is likely to stem from their own childhood experiences of deprivation and abuse which they have rigorously repressed over the years; and this will be the case whether their attitude is one of overt hostility towards the victim or superficial emotional identification with the victim. In our experience, once a perpetrator has felt himself to be heard as a victim in his own right (in terms of his own early experiences), then he has a better emotional capacity for contemplating his own victim's feelings.

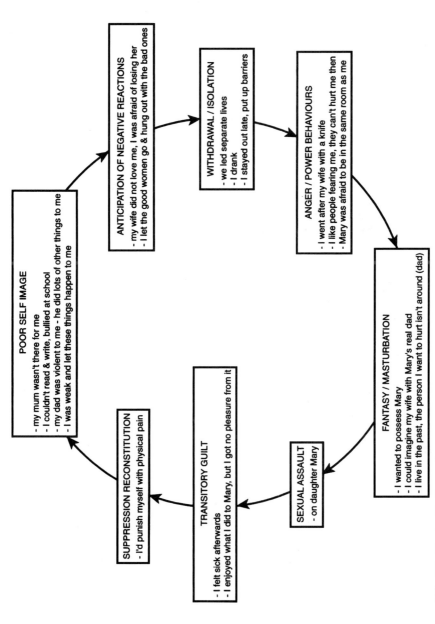

POOR SELF IMAGE
- my mum wasn't there for me
- I couldn't read & write, bullied at school
- my dad was violent to me - he did lots of other things to me
- I was weak and let these things happen to me

ANTICIPATION OF NEGATIVE REACTIONS
- my wife did not love me, I was afraid of losing her
- I let the good women go & hung out with the bad ones

WITHDRAWAL / ISOLATION
- we led separate lives
- I drank
- I stayed out late, put up barriers

ANGER / POWER BEHAVIOURS
- I went after my wife with a knife
- I like people fearing me, they can't hurt me then
- Mary was afraid to be in the same room as me

FANTASY / MASTURBATION
- I wanted to possess Mary
- I could imagine my wife with Mary's real dad
- I live in the past, the person I want to hurt isn't around (dad)

SEXUAL ASSAULT
- on daughter Mary

TRANSITORY GUILT
- I felt sick afterwards
- I enjoyed what I did to Mary, but I got no pleasure from it

SUPPRESSION RECONSTITUTION
- I'd punish myself with physical pain

FIG. 6.3 Tom's offending cycle.

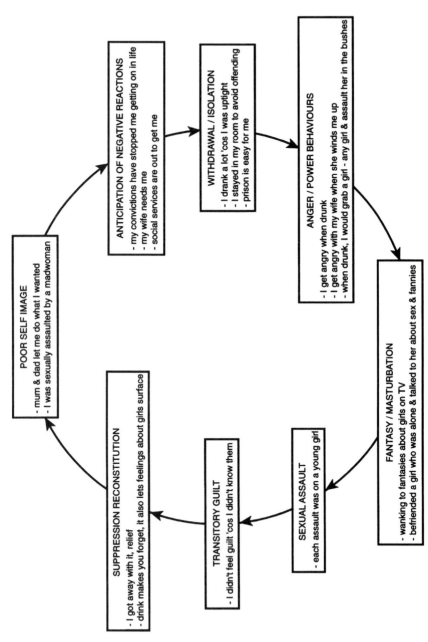

FIG. 6.4 Peter's offending cycle.

Initially group members are instructed to recall a single non sexual memory of an event in childhood when he was victimised. Common themes are bullying, humiliations, physical assaults, or gross neglect. They are then encouraged in pairs to relate their stories in terms of what happened, thoughts and feelings, feeding back each other's experiences. During the subsequent session, another memory is elicited of an incident of victimisation, but this time when the group member managed to emerge victorious against his aggressor. In this way, victim experiences are noted as well as specific feelings surrounding the reversal of the situation, such as triumph, exhilaration, fear, and anger. The process of retrieving painful memories and relating them to an interested and supportive group is, in itself, a significant therapeutic process which can be developed in individual supervision sessions.

The theme of the sessions shifts to issues of sexual abuse, and material is shown of young male victims talking about their experiences. We chose to show the television programme on Castle Hill in which four or five adolescent boys talk articulately and painfully about the cycle of bullying and sexual abuse instigated by the headmaster of a boarding school for boys with learning and behavioural problems. This creates a forum in which further sessions can be devoted to the group members' own sexual victimisation experiences. Member are split into small groups, pairing an abused with a non-abused group member, and the discussion is carefully controlled to explore the following questions:

1. Why me?
2. What effect did it have on me?
3. Why was I unable to stop it, or to disclose it?
4. How did I feel about the perpetrator then, and now?

It should be emphasised that the group does not provide a forum in which to resolve victimisation experiences, and gratuitous accounts of detailed sexual acts should be avoided. Victimised group members should be allowed to disclose as little as they wish, in order to address the above questions; the aim is to develop links between the abused and abuser aspects of the group member. Nevertheless, this can often be an emotional time, and referrers should be kept informed of the situation and group members encouraged to talk further in individual supervision.

In the final sessions, all group members are asked to write letters to their own perpetrator, detailing what occurred and the impact it had on them, at the time and subsequently. The letters—completed and revised as homework tasks—are read out by the group member to an empty chair.

Tom's letter to his step-father:

"You stole my innocence, everything you showed me and taught me was wrong, the cuddles and affection you gave me was all an act, you made me believe you loved me, I needed someone to love me, but it ended the same way as always you just used me.

When I was at school no one wanted to know me. I wanted to do things to them that you taught me, I told them things they didn't want to know, so I was an outcast, children I had known for years wouldn't even talk to me, it was so lonely.

Because of you I have grown up taking what I wanted without any thought for the person I was taking it from, I hate you but not as much as I hate myself.

I have got to try and live with myself, I don't know if I can, but I am going to try, because otherwise it means I am totally worthless and I hope I can disprove that.

Why me? Why not my brother or sister? No I don't mean that I wouldn't wish that on them.

I'm glad you died young. I hope you suffered, I know you wanted your own children—a son. I'm glad you couldn't have any, I hope you suffered about that every day of your miserable life.
Tom."

George, who was also very seriously abused, was unable to acknowledge for months in therapy the way he was used for sexual gratification by the adults and then discarded. He clung to the idea that he sought and was therefore responsible for the sexual contact, and that his surrogate "mother and father" were primarily loving. It was only later that he was able to acknowledge the intense loneliness of returning to an empty home after being videoed, and washing the blood off his anus and pants, knowing that there was no one to ask where he had been.

Homework.   See above.

Relationships

Aim.   To elicit repeated patterns in relationships with others, including dysfunctional attitudes, and to highlight the difficulties in sustaining intimate relationships.

Content.   Relationships are traced back to early experiences of being parented; a discussion of the group members' perception of mother and father's characteristics is based around completion of the Parental Bonding Questionnaire (Parker, Tupling, & Brown, 1979) (Fig. 6.5). Sexual development, learning about sex and the experiences of puberty can provide a more lighthearted group, and literature or film material can be used. On the whole, sexual knowledge is usually adequate, but deficits should be communicated to the referrer, and an education package completed if necessary.

"First love" forms the theme of another session, as so many of the perpetrators recall an early idealised infatuation, in which sex played an irrelevant or subsidiary role. For others, they will present an experience of sexual victimisation,

Answer the questions as you remember your parents in your first sixteen years.
Please put a tick in the column which describes them as they were

My mother / father (delete as appropriate)

	Very similar to	Quite similar to	Not very similar to	Not at all similar to
1 Spoke to me with a warm and friendly voice				
2 Helped me as much as I needed				
3 Let me do things I liked doing				
4 Seemed emotionally cold to me				
5 Appeared to understand my problems and worries				
6 Was affectionate to me				
7 Liked me to make my own decisions				
8 Wanted me to grow up				
9 Tried to control everything I did				
10 Invaded my privacy				
11 Enjoyed talking things over with me				
12 Frequently smiled at me				
13 Tended to baby me				
14 Seemed to understand what I needed or wanted				
15 Let me decide things for myself				
16 Made me feel I wasn't wanted				
17 Could make me feel better when I was upset				
18 Talked to me often				
19 Tried to make me dependent on her / him				
20 Felt that I could not look after myself unless she / he was around				
21 Gave me as much freedom as I wanted				
22 Let me go out as often as I wanted				
23 Was overprotective of me				
24 Praised me				
25 Let me dress in any way I pleased				

FIG. 6.5 Parental bonding questionnaire (Parker et al., 1979).

apparently incomprehending of any emotional connection with others which has not been overtly sexualised. This was the case for Peter, who presented his experience of being encouraged to fantasise about girls in the swimming pool, alongside an older boy of 19, as his first attempts at "relationships".

Subsequent sessions address experiences in adulthood: the majority of perpetrators in the group are heterosexual in orientation and have had at least one sexual relationship, but care should be taken to include homosexual relationships and those perpetrators who have never experienced intimate contact with another adult. Group members are encouraged to explore their assumptions and attitudes in relating to women, and to articulate their perceptions of disappointments, betrayals and rejections. It is important to deflect the group away from a collusive shift of blame onto partners, and to encourage them at all times to challenge each other's own contributions to their difficulties: it is essential for the group members to recognise why they were attracted to certain individuals, and what it was in their behaviour—alcohol use, possessiveness, working hours, lack of emotional expression, fear of dependency or abandonment, sexual preoccupation or withdrawal—which may have pushed their partner away (or led to a complete avoidance of relationships).

Patterns in relating from childhood through to adulthood should be drawn together, and key themes added to the offending cycle.

Victim awareness

Aim.   To develop both an intellectual understanding of the impact of victimisation on children, and an emotional insight into the distressing nature of the experience—applying it to their own victim—with particular reference to issues of consent and compliance.

Content.   Facing possible victim distress and emotional damage clearly raises considerable anxieties in perpetrators, and it may be advisable to commence this module with a more intellectual and non-personalised discussion, using written or filmed material of victims (often adult survivors) talking about their experiences. It is, of course, important to ensure that all potentially "titillating" material is removed, and that thoughts and feelings are emphasised, or such material will take on a pornographic aspect in the perpetrator's mind. We have also introduced a debating session based on the four key questions addressed in Abel, Becker, and Cunningham-Rathner's (1984) paper on informed consent in child sexual abuse victims: does the child understand what she consents to; is the child aware of the accepted sexual standards in her community; does the child appreciate the eventual, possible consequences of the decision; and are the child and the adult equally powerful so that no coercion influences the child's decision? This task enables not only fixated perpetrators' attitudes to be challenged, but also the more subtle distortions of other perpetrators who, for example, emphasise the sexually provocative nature of 12-year-olds, or the absence of overt force as a mitigating factor.

Subsequent sessions revolve around key homework tasks: writing an imaginary letter from the group member's victim to himself; and writing a victim apology letter. Both tasks may require recourse to the victim statements, in order to emphasise certain aspects of the victim's experience. The first task should outline the nature of the victim's experience, the effect of the abuse on the victim, why the victim could not stop it or disclose it, and what the victim would wish to say now to their perpetrator. As such it is an exercise in perspective-taking which can make use of what has been learnt intellectually at a general level, what has been learnt about the emotional impact of abuse, and any personal information available about the perpetrator's victim. The second task must address issues such as the perpetrator taking full responsibility for the abuse and its consequences, a statement that the victim was not to blame and was right to disclose, and an unequivocal apology.

Kevin's letter from Sally to himself:

> "Dear . . .
> I wrote this letter to tell you how I felt. I wish now that you had stopped me from rubbing myself on top of you and putting your hands down my trousers. When I used to pull the curtains together in the living room, I suppose I must have got some kind of thrill. I know that when you used to get excited, your pants became wet when you used to go to the bathroom. You never touched me like Grandad did, but I knew that what was happening was wrong. I seem to have been driven by some kind of force. I can't explain. it's so sad what happened. You made my life so safe after Peter had gone. Why did this happen? I know you hated granny but I told her everything one night when she was bathing me. I was thinking of telling Mum but I didn't. The last time it happened I didn't wear any knickers under my dressing gown, I don't know why. Yours truly, Sally"

Kevin wrote this letter early on in treatment when he is clearly firmly entrenched in the view that the abuse was encouraged—at the very least—by Sally, that she held sad rather than angry feelings about what occurred, and that his behaviour could not be compared to the seriously assaultative behaviour which the grandfather had allegedly perpetrated. He responded to rather negative group feedback by saying,

> "I just think that if I had stopped her . . . if I had stopped her from day one. That is what I regret now. There is something within that girl—I am not blaming Sally at all—I think it's from grandad . . . (long pause) I knew no-one would believe me."

Tom's letter from Mary to himself:

> "I was a normal happy little girl, I loved my mum, dad (step-dad), brother, I used to go with dad on his ice cream van. When mum left, dad changed, he made me wear my mum's clothes and started doing things to me I didn't like. He kept me up late at night and made me sit on his lap. The girls at school didn't like me anymore, but the boys did, I started to get into more trouble at school, I wouldn't do my homework and kept bunking off.
>
> I hated what you did to me dad, you made me suck your willy, it was horrible, it tasted nasty. You wanted me to play with it, you made me, why dad? Why did you do it, why did you pick on me? Daddies don't do that to their children (you made me believe they did). You said I was special, I didn't want to be I just wanted to be your daughter. It used to make me sick to suck your willy and you knew it but you still expected me to want to do it. I did it because you were my dad and I loved you, but also because I was terrified of you. I was too scared to tell you that you were hurting me. When I told, why wasn't I believed? Why didn't you own up, it could have ended three years earlier.
> Mary"

Although Tom has made a fairly good attempt at understanding his step-daughter's feelings, it is striking to compare the emotional quality of the letter (the hostility being directed towards his behaviour, not particularly towards himself) with his letter to his own perpetrators which seethes with anger and bitterness.

Victim apology; interestingly, **Peter** felt unable to write a letter, but read a statement out to the group:

> "I can only say that they must have gone through the worst times of their lives. The trust was broken that they had in adults, the emotion that a stranger has invaded the most private parts of their body, the frightening time that I had put them through. They must feel their childhood was stolen . . . That's all I can think of"

The group responded by pointing out the lack of feeling in his comments, and his avoidance of thinking about one victim in particular. Peter responded by saying:

> "Most of my victims—the whole assault takes minutes. I can't get into the person. My victims are not people to me, they are just someone to get my rocks off there and then, and I've gone"

Homework.   See letter writing tasks above.

Offending cycle

Aim.   To introduce the concept of relapse prevention, identifying high risk situations and emotions outlined on the offence cycle, and to prepare for realistically appraising the future.

Content.   This module makes no attempt to cover the full range of relapse prevention strategies, but can emphasise possible risks. There are two main components: firstly, to update and amend group members' offence cycles in the light of all that has been discussed in the group sessions. This can then lead to the identification of weak points in the cycle for each perpetrator. Attention must be drawn again, where appropriate, to the role of fantasy in breaking down resistance to re-offending. Secondly, group members are asked to complete a decision matrix regarding the positive and negative, short and long-term consequences of offending. At this late stage in the group, members are often tempted to emphasise the negative aspects of offending, which can be unhelpful if they are to face up to what is being relinquished. It is unlikely that they will easily find alternatives to the short-lived but intense gratification which abuse can bring to a perpetrator.

Kevin's decision matrix is outlined in Fig. 6.6.

Homework.   Both adding to the offence cycle, and developing and amending the decision matrix are homework tasks in this module.

Offending disclosure

Aim.   To review progress in terms of disclosure, residual denial and distortions, the degree of understanding of motivations and process which facilitated and maintained the offending behaviour.

Content.   The final session for any group member should include a review of his original disclosure—as recorded on video or flipchart. The group member has an opportunity to add to or amend what has been said, and other group members are encouraged to participate. This allows an opportunity for a group discussion of the perpetrator's progress in treatment, and areas of weakness remaining. Feedback from both therapists and group members must be constructive and forward-looking. The group members' capacity to express warm feelings of support and appropriate feedback, are indicators of their capacity for an empathic and mature response. Group members differ in the extent to which they are able to express their ambivalence about leaving: the relief with which they perceive treatment to be "over" is likely to be tempered with a sense of loss and isolation as their membership of a clearly identifiable group ceases.

	SHORT-TERM CONSEQUENCES		LONG-TERM CONSEQUENCES	
	Positive	**Negative**	**Positive**	**Negative**
TO OFFEND	• sexual pleasure • exciting • safe • no pressure to perform • live out fantasies • innocent • all mine—possession	• fear of being caught • daughter wouldn't come to me • self-disgust • not being able to stop—knowing I should • addictive	• always available • good memories of abuse to fantasise about • total control • thought that it would last forever—saw no end to it	• loss of family for victim & self • fear—who's next • feeling out of control • can't allow children close, but wanting to • not wanting / being able to stop
NOT TO OFFEND	• I'm free • no guilt • relief I've been caught • feeling better about me as not offending	• sexually frustrated • learn to control & change the fantasy • wishing I'd not been caught • missing the excitement	• daughter wants to stay in contact • easier to live with self • children are safer • my children still love me	• fear of repetition rules to live by • no fantasies / control masturbation • live with memories of what I've done • can't allow kids close • no relief from fantasies • bad feels good & good feels bad • missing offending

FIG. 6.6 Kevin's decision matrix.

PROGRESS IN TREATMENT

Tom's progress in therapy was coloured by his irritation at the other men not being honest. He would castigate himself to the point where leaders were concerned about his wellbeing, and they (and group members) would refrain from pushing him on areas he found difficult. His apparent honesty was contrasted by his rather seductive references to "things my dad did". He was a powerful member of the group who controlled others by a quiet menace or by the dreadful frankness of his offending accounts or own victim experiences. He was always cooperative with homework tasks, and participated fully in the sessions. Despite low levels of denial or distorted attitudes towards his victim and his offending, it was clear that he found it impossible to develop emotionally to the point where he could lay the past to rest. He continued to attend after his parole ended for some weeks, but dropped out after the Easter break, during which time his ex-wife remarried.

Peter's behaviour in therapy was coloured by his need to take control, and thereby sabotage any threat of intimacy within the group. He was sometimes late, and smelt of alcohol on three occasions. He encouraged talk of fantasies, and reverted to sexualised discussion whenever asked about his feelings. Otherwise he dominated open discussion with his current "victim-isation" by social services. His compliance with homework tasks was poor. The therapists became more adept at ignoring sexual comments and always drawing him out on feelings, although the battle for control was a constant dynamic. However after missing 1 session (with an excuse), warnings for lateness, and behaving aggressively to the therapists when under the influence of alcohol, he was discharged from the group.

George entered individual therapy for one year, followed by monthly follow-up for one year. He was fully committed and became quite dependent on the therapist who represented the available and consistent mother that he had never had. Themes in therapy were mourning the loss of the idea of a loving relationship with the victim, and thus gradually accepting the reality of the abuse. George was much more comfortable discussing the offence—appropriately—than recalling his own unhappy family life or the pornography ring into which he was seduced. Acknowledging his own experience of being buggered immediately resulted in a strong desire to seek comfort by masturbating a boy, as he travelled from that session to his home. The theme of grieving was continued as he relinquished the idealised substitute family of his childhood, and acknowledged some of his anger at being used and physically hurt, his neediness for his mother which he had previously denied, and his fear of and anger towards women.

Kevin settled well into the group, despite considerable initial denial. If directly challenged, he reverted to his "victim" position, but generally he participated in an active fashion. His contributions were very self-preoccupied and rambling for the first few months, which had the effect of irritating and alienating therapists and group members alike who ceased to listen to him, thus reinforcing his perception of himself as a victim. However, when the therapists were able to identify and point out his behaviour, he responded well and improved his listening skills and his contributions to others. He learned to talk about his feelings of inadequacy, and the element of anger and revenge in his offending behaviour. He appeared to benefit from the sharing of experiences and general supportive attention, which appeared to be as instrumental in reducing his denial and distortions, as the educative components of the programme.

RELAPSE PREVENTION

Definition

Relapse prevention (RP) is a self-control programme designed to teach individuals who are trying to change their behaviour how to anticipate and cope with the problem of relapse. As Marlatt (1982) originally described, RP is designed to enhance maintenance of change of compulsive behaviours over time and across situations. Clearly, for the sex offender, successful maintenance is the attainment of long-term abstinence in regard to the performance of unlawful sexual acts. Based on social cognitive principles, RP has a psychoeducational thrust that combines behavioural skill-training procedures with cognitive intervention techniques (George & Marlatt, 1989).

There are certain critical assumptions about addictive disorders in relation to the relapse prevention model, which distinguishes it from the medical-disease theoretical model in the addictions field. Firstly, addictive behaviour patterns are seen as multiply-determined by early learning experiences, situational antecedents, prevailing contingencies of reward and punishment, cognitive beliefs, and biological influences; secondly, the target behaviour is best understood as lying on a continuum between nonproblematic and problematic expression; thirdly, the addictive behaviour can be conceptualised as a maladaptive response for coping with life stressors.

Whether child sexual abuse can be considered an addictive behaviour, is unclear. Certainly there are similarities with other addictions, in that sexual assaults yeld immediate short-term satisfaction for the offender in the form of an explosive release of feelings and decreased tension, but the long-term consequences are profoundly negative and tension inducing; and sexual offending clearly results in excessive personal and social costs. However clear differences lie in the victimisation involved in sexual offending which emphasises the grave consequences to any and each relapse in the behaviour; the fact that relapse involves an illegal act; and the importance of fantasy life in the sexual offender which may afford greater gratification (including physiological arousal) than fantasy in other addictions. Furthermore, a RP addiction model is in danger of ignoring real differences in motivations, deviant arousal levels, and relapse rates between perpetrators of child sexual abuse. Nevertheless, the RP emphasis on enhancing personal responsibility and self-control is central to work with perpetrators, and RP strategies can legitimately be employed in treatment, whether or not the behaviour of the perpetrator is construed as an addiction (George & Marlatt, 1989).

Precursors to relapse

Pithers, Buell, Kashima, Cumming, and Beal (1987) analysed precursors to the offences of 136 child molesters and 64 rapists, including multiple determinants in an attempt to identify a relapse process occurring over a long period of time. They were able to highlight a common sequence of changes ultimately leading to reoffending: the first change was affective (a deterioration in emotional state); the second change involved fantasies of performing the deviant sexual act; fantasies were subsequently turned into thoughts involving cognitive distortions or "thinking errors"; passive planning ensued in which they would cognitively refine the circumstances that would permit commission of a sexual offence (often accomplished during masturbatory fantasies); and finally, the plan was acted out behaviourally.

Theoretical concepts

High risk situations (HRS). A HRS can be defined as any situation that poses a threat to perceived control and thereby increases the probability of lapse or relapse. The probability of relapse is then a function of (1) the extent to which the individual feels helpless in relation to the influence of others or external events; (2) the immediate availability of a coping response as an alternative to the dysfunctional behaviour in a high-risk situation; (3) an individual's expectations about the consequences of the behavioural alternatives in the risk situation; and (4) the availability of victims (opportunity) (Pithers et al., 1987).

"Apparently irrelevant decision" (AID). Marlatt and Gordon (1980) identified the subtle and progressive series of approach behaviours to HRS, distorted or obscured by rationalisations and denial, and called them "apparently irrelevant decisions". Common AIDs in perpetrators of child sexual abuse will include vocational and recreational decisions, relationship decisions, decisions to frequent high-risk places, and decisions to assist and befriend.

Lapses and relapses. A relapse is quite simply defined as a return to sexually aggressive behaviours, including any single violation of the rule. Lapses are defined early in the preoffence chain as any occurrence of wilful and elaborate fantasising about sexual offending or any sources of stimulation associated with the sexual offence pattern.

Abstinence violation effect (AVE). The significance of the abstinence violation effect lies in its capacity to facilitate the escalation of a lapse into a relapse (Marlatt, 1985). There are two sources to AVE: firstly the potential conflict between a perpetrator's previous self-image as an abstainer and his recent experience of a lapse, accompanied by feelings of discomfort, which may be resolved by indulgence in the forbidden behaviour to counteract the uncomfortable emotional state or realign the self-image with the discrepant behaviour; secondly, AVE may be triggered to the extent that the individual views a lapse as a personal (internal) failure, thus promoting relapse via a self-fulfilling prophecy whereby expectations for continued failure will increase.

Assessment procedures

Much of the preliminary assessment work for RP is outlined in Chapters three and six. Two tasks remain which are specifically RP focused:

Analysis of the perpetrator's high-risk situations, including "apparently irrelevant decisions".   The information should be available to some extent in the detailed offence cycle completed in the core treatment programme. However, continued assessment can take place in terms of ongoing self-monitoring—a diary which records sequences of events, feelings, fantasies, and thoughts on a daily basis.

Assessment of the perpetrator's skills for coping with the identified high-risk situations.   Techniques could include self-efficacy ratings where an individual is asked to rate the ease with which he would cope with a specific set of high-risk situations. For the perpetrator with good imagery skills, lapse fantasies (hypothetical lapse situations) can be developed, and the range of adaptive and maladaptive coping responses noted.

Interventions

Detailed accounts of RP programmes for sexual offenders can be found in Salter (1988) and Laws (1989). Programmes will need to address the following areas.

Risk recognition

This should include identifying high risk situations and the recognition of AIDs, and lifestyle imbalances which may be precursors to a HRS. Lifestyle imbalances refer to discrepancies between duties and obligations in life on the one hand, and indulgences on the other; perpetrators may be encouraged to find substitute indulgences and positive addictions to replace the short-term gratifications afforded by their previous offending behaviour.

Avoiding lapses

This may include stimulus control procedures (avoiding pertinent cues from the perpetrator's surroundings), avoidance and/or escape strategies (where speed of response is more important than the "optimal" coping response). Lapse and relapse rehearsal are essential tools in the RP programme, and role play may help to consolidate learning. Coping with urges may need to be addressed, particularly when a perpetrator selectively recalls the positive effects of past offences, and has a high positive outcome expectancy for the immediate effects of a behaviour when faced with a HRS. The decision matrix can offer a perspective in these situations (see Chapter six) and the perpetrator should be told that urges can be "surfed" like waves, that they will always subside with time and do not have to be acted upon.

Minimising the extent of lapses

The first and most essential intervention is to introduce the concept of lapse as extremely likely at some point in the future, in order to enhance the perpetrator's control over the negative influence of the AVE when a lapse does occur. Contracting will allow for the limitations to lapses to be clearly laid out between perpetrator and therapist; lapses are reconceptualised as slips or mistakes which do not equate with total loss of control but are learning situations for the perpetrator; guilty feelings should be anticipated and reassurance given; and finally a series of escape strategies should be available to the perpetrator. Many programmes issue their clients with maintenance manuals which can be carried around at all times.

CHALLENGE PROJECT RELAPSE PREVENTION PROGRAMME

The Challenge Project relapse prevention programme was designed to complement and enhance the core programme. It was based on the following premises:

1. Sexual offending is not an impulsive behaviour.
2. Certain identifiable risk ractors will be present for each offender in the future.
3. Identification and management of these factors can prevent re-offending.

The group structure was to meet weekly, for eight to ten weeks (depending upon number of group members), for one and a half hours. The therapists comprise a forensic psychologist, and a sex offender specialist probation officer.

Group membership was open to all men living in the catchment area who had sexually offended (convicted or unconvicted) against children. It was essential that all the members had previously completed a personal offending cycle, either as part of the Challenge core programme, the prison sex offender treatment programme, and/or individual work with a probation officer/other therapist. This was the minimum requirement, although wherever possible, members were encouraged to complete an intensive treatment programme as a prerequisite.

The group members are given a personal notebook in which to record their learning in the group and complete homework tasks.

As with the core programme, communication with the referrer and relevant agencies is open, and final RP reports are written which indicate progress, areas of concern and recommended focus of future work. The group member is allowed to comment upon the report, and to receive a copy.

Content

Session 1: Introduction. Discussion of contractual "rules" (see core programme), homework expectations, reasons for attending, hopes and fears. Homework involves self-monitoring in diary format for this and subsequent sessions.

Sessions 2 and 3: Offending cycles. Presentation and discussion of group members" offending cycles, highlighting antecedents to their assaults.

Session 4: Lapses, relapses and high risk situations. RP model outlined and discussed, with examples drawn from group members" offending cycles. Homework includes development of a relapse fantasy relating to the situation in which they would feel most at risk.

Session 5: Relapse fantasy. Relapse fantasies are broken down into affective, cognitive and behavioural components, as well as highlighting the series of discrete steps and stages where coping strategies may be employed. Homework includes identifying strategies for coping with each stage of the lapse/relapse cycle.

Session 6: Techniques for dealing with relapse. Coping strategies for lapses and relapses are discussed, elaborated and, if need be, role-played.

Session 7: Thinking errors. The concept of thinking errors is explained, and the group splits into pairs to identify dangerous personal cognitive distortions and AIDs. Self-statements are generated to counter these. Homework follows an explanation of lifestyle imbalance in the group session, and entails keeping a diary for the week listing "shoulds" and "wants".

Session 8: Achieving lifestyle balance. Homework is fed back, and the group splits into pairs in order to discuss how to plan a shift in lifestyle balance. Homework requires group members to prepare a summary of what they have learned from the group and how they will apply this to avoiding future offending.

Session 9: Ending. Group members are encouraged to talk about their feelings regarding the ending. Feedback is given on the homework and simple maintenance manuals are devised which the group members can employ in high risk or lapse situations.

In summary, one established programme in southeast London has been presented, which comprises both an intensive and a relapse prevention group treatment format. Many readers might prefer to alter the emphasis and/or format suggested and Chapter seven describes in some detail the issues involved in the evaluation of a treatment programme. However, it must be remembered that it is difficult to quantify the impact of organisational features and non-specific therapist qualities which should not be discarded in the attempt to cover current thinking on programme content.

The evaluation of treatment programmes

THE PURPOSE OF EVALUATION

To a few—usually those from a scientist–practitioner background—the purpose and need for evaluation is self-evident. For many, evaluation is something left to others, something which may result in the deployment of scarce resources away from treatment provision, something rather intangible and forbidding, or —at worst—something which could dent confidence in a lovingly constructed programme. Perhaps the first question that should be asked of oneself and close colleagues is, "could I/we bear to find out that treatment does not work?" If this possibility, however remote, can be contemplated, then the threat of evaluation becomes more manageable.

The need for evaluation of sex offender treatment programmes is particularly acute, not least because such approaches on a large scale are relatively new, and good methodological studies are rare. In other words, and as outlined below in this chapter, there is not yet any conclusive evidence that treatment always "works" for all sexual offenders. As practitioners involved in assessing risk, recommending and implementing treatment in a variety of settings, we have a professional duty to know what we are recommending, why we are doing so, and what are the likely outcomes and risks to the public. These ethical standards are particularly pertinent when considering the release of high risk sex offenders from custody into the community, or when advising child protection agencies whether a perpetrator may or may not safely return to the family home. One serious mistake can have enormous ramifications which perhaps eradicate public confidence in a programme, particularly if the media takes an interest. The judiciary themselves take risks in acceding to requests to impose community sentences involving treatment packages, and they do so on the basis that the practitioners involved hold expert knowledge regarding the likelihood of success.

Nevertheless, evaluation should not simply be considered a defensive exercise within a hostile environment. Demonstrating that treatment can be effective is probably the most substantial means of maintaining self-respect and general morale amongst programme managers and therapists. It is probably the most powerful tool in retaining the interest of budget-holders and, as such, essential to the survival and development of programmes.

As practitioners, we are likely to have a number of more clinically relevant questions (some of which are beginning to be answered), which would help us to prioritise and target scarce resources:

1. Does treatment provide an significant reduction in reoffending below the untreated reconviction rate for perpetrators, which takes into account known differences between targeted gender of victim, and relationship to the perpetrator? (See Chapter three for information on risk prediction.)
2. Does treatment reduce the number of future victims, delay offending, or reduce the degree of physical/emotional harm victims endure?
3. Do we know which type of sexual offender responds to treatment, and can responders (versus non-responders) be differentiated by offence type, historical details or psychological characteristics?
4. Do we know what model of treatment is most effective, what the key components of that model may be, and whether there are identifiable exceptions to this who may need an alternative treatment package?

It would probably be fair to say currently, that the vast majority of treatment programmes in Britain for perpetrators of child sexual abuse are based on a cognitive–behavioural approach, largely derivative from American and Canadian programmes. As Barker and Beech (1993) conclude in their appraisal of probation led programmes, there has been "the wholesale adoption of cognitive–behavioural therapy, and a largely uncritical acceptance of groupwork as the medium through which it is done. The reality in this country is that its efficacy remains largely untested ..." (p. 42). Even at the most simplistic evaluation level, it is likely that a significant number of group programmes fail to collect follow-up data, or to measure psychological changes before and after treatment.

OUTCOME STUDIES

There are key papers within the academic journals which usefully review the empirical studies of sex offender recidivism and address the question of treatment efficacy. The arguments are summarised by Furby, Weinrott, and Blackshaw (1989), Quinsey, Harris, Rice, and Lalumiere (1993), and Marshall and Pithers (1994), details of which are outlined here.

Furby et al. (1989)

Furby et al. accumulated a comprehensive review of empirical sex offender recidivism studies going back to the 1960s. The review was exhaustive, including both treated and untreated sex offender studies. However they did exclude studies with a sample size of less than 10 subjects (in order to avoid the bias towards favourable outcomes inherent in single case study reports), and excluded studies which did not include official records in their outcome data. Having made a substantial number of methodological criticisms of the studies, they rather depressingly conclude:

1. There is no evidence that treatment reduces the rates of sex offences generally, nor is there any evidence for assessing whether treatment may be differentially effective for different types of offender.
2. There is some evidence that recidivism rates may be different for different types of offenders.
3. The longer the follow-up period, the greater the percentage of men who reoffend—although not necessarily sexually.

They raise the question of whether it is possible to project long-term recidivism from short-term data, and recommend that follow-up take place for at least 10 years.

Marshall and Pithers (1994)

Marshall and Pithers are altogether more confident, having conducted their own evaluation studies with colleagues which suggested greater success. They pointed out that many of the treatment models reviewed by Furby were obsolete at the time of publication, and many utilised outdated treatment approaches. They highlight methodological flaws including the duplication of data and potential biases against treatment effects. Marques, Day, Nelson, and West (1994) echo this criticism, pointing out that Furby's discouraging conclusions are not based on solid findings of treatment effectiveness, but on the basis that conclusions about treatment effects could not be drawn. Marshall and Pithers also respond to sceptical reports by the Penetanguishene group in evaluating their own programmes (Rice, Quinsey & Harris, 1991) by suggesting that their treatment was overly reliant on altering deviant sexual preferences, the specific components of the programme were inadequate, and their offender population highly disturbed.

Marshall, Jones, Ward, Johnston, and Barbaree (1991) evaluated their outpatient treatment programmes for child molesters, utilising both official and unofficial police and child protection agency records. Treated subjects were carefully matched on various offence and demographic features with subjects who also sought treatment but were unable to enter the programme. They found that all subgroups of child molester who were treated had significantly lower reoffence rates than did their untreated counterparts. In their review, they conclude:

1. The roles of treatment provider and treatment evaluator should be separated out to avoid a conflict of interest.
2. "Overcontrolled" outcome studies necessarily result in an underestimation of actual treatment efficacy; interventions must be responsive to the client's changing needs over time.
3. We have a moral obligation to offer treatment to as many clients as possible, even if we are unable to identify who will respond effectively, and therefore random allocation to a no-treatment group (see below) is not justifiable: withholding treatment may result in the emotional/physical injury of an innocent other who was not able to give consent to the research design.

Quinsey et al. (1993)

Quinsey et al. criticise Marshall et al.'s 1991 review of treatment outcome, on the following issues.

Quinsey et al. propose that psychologists (and other practitioners) have an ethical obligation to reduce the present ambiguity about the effects of sex offender treatment, and thus random design studies including a no-treatment group are ethically justifiable.

They suggest that a reliance—for comparison groups—on an estimate of the likely outcome in the absence of treatment based on information about subjects' histories of criminal and sexual offending is unsatisfactory: it is difficult to infer untreated recidivism rates from the literature because the rates vary tremendously across studies. Groups of subjects explicitly matched on risk are only comparable if the groups are sampled from the same time period, and locality.

Thirdly, they point to the potential overestimate of treatment effectiveness caused by not considering those who refuse treatment and drop-outs when comparing the outcomes of those who complete treatment with the outcomes of untreated men: Marques et al. (1994) found five times the rate of new sexual reoffending for treatment drop-outs in comparison with treated, volunteer and non-voluntary control groups; Owen and Steele (1991, cited in Fisher & Thornton, 1993) reported that 25% of incest offenders dropping out of treatment sexually reoffended in comparison with 5% of those completing treatment.

METHODOLOGICAL CONCERNS

Furby et al. (1989) provide the most comprehensive breakdown of the key methodological problems encountered in sex offender research, and many of their points are reiterated by authors mentioned earlier.

Sample selection and description

In order to be able to generalise results, any evaluation study needs to define its sample very carefully, addressing issues such as demographic variables, criminal history, type of psychosexual disorder, the victim characteristics, legal status, amenability to treatment (voluntary versus non-voluntary), community and family supports.

Study design

A prospective study allows for an assessment battery, including clinical interview details and psychometric tests, to be administered, before and preferably after treatment. Retrospective studies are reliant on recorded data, much of which can be inadequate, and follow-up of individuals can be difficult, particularly as they have not already given permission to participate in research. Nevertheless, retrospective studies are less time consuming and resource intensive, and may provide useful preliminary information prior to designing a prospective study.

Single group versus multiple group studies

The central problem with single group studies is that it is almost impossible to measure effectiveness without some sort of comparison group or data, unless the recidivism rate is either 0% or 100%. Most studies attempt to provide comparison data, often utilising published recidivism rates (subject to the problems cited earlier). Previous offending rates for the single group design are rarely useful because they are low, and historical factors may bear an influence. Preferably, there should be the simultaneous comparison between two groups, which employs either the random allocation of subjects to research group, or matching subjects across groups on key variables implicated in sex offender recidivism.

Evaluating treatment effectiveness

The ethical dilemmas posed by a no-treatment control group have been outlined earlier. Certainly, subjects must not be allocated on the basis of motivation, or their offending behaviour. Furthermore, much of the value of establishing treatment effectiveness is lost if the nature of the intervention is not made clear: it is essential to be aware of the components of treatment, the order in which they were delivered, and the degree to which therapists were known to deviate from protocols, that is to say, treatment integrity (Hollin, 1995). The aims of treatment should be made entirely explicit, so that the measures chosen for evaluation purposes match the objectives.

Sample size

A recidivism study should comprise a sample of sufficient size to conduct appropriate statistical tests of comparisons within or between studies. Failures need to be carefully defined, the length of follow-up explicit, record sources to be checked, the drop-out rate, and the anticipated impact of any intervention detailed.

Criteria measured

Clearly a definition of recidivism is required, the most obvious being the reconviction for further sexual offences. Quinsey et al. (1993) concur with Marshall et al. (1991) in endorsing the use of official police records of sexual offences as the measure of outcome: for all their shortcomings, they are less subject to bias than any other available outcome measure. In addition, data on non-sexual reoffending can be crucial, particularly in considering violent recidivism and the impact of the police or Crown Prosecution Service reducing or dropping charges in order to secure a conviction. For this reason, sexual recidivism is best measured from actual offence descriptions, rather than the charge sheets. Additional information may be accessed by police and child protection agency records.

Operational measures

Having established that recidivism information should be based on multiple sources, summary statistics should be compiled on the raw data. At its most simplistic level, this can include the percentage of subjects who reoffend at least once during a specified follow-up period, where the follow-up period is uniform for all subjects. The life-table method (cited in Furby et al., 1989) is a more accurate way of calculating the likelihood of subjects reoffending during a specified follow-up period, and allows for different follow-up start times: the percentage of subjects who first relapsed during their first year at risk is calculated, and they are removed in calculating the percentage of subjects who first relapsed during their second year at risk, and so on for subsequent years at risk; the cumulative total percentage can then be determined for any given time period at risk.

Data analysis

Attrition—disappearance of the original sample due to relocation, record loss and name change—is an inevitable problem in a longitudinal study, and all the more problematic when there is a reliance on contact with the offender, not just his records.

RECENT TREATMENT EFFECTIVENESS STUDIES

The following three outcome studies have been summarised here in order to explore the recent attempts to evaluate treatment programmes in Britain (STEP Project and Challenge Project), and to demonstrate a well thought out and robust methodological design (Marques et al., 1994).

Marques et al. (1994)

Marques and colleagues have published preliminary findings of the Sex Offender Treatment and Evaluation Project (SOTEP) which targets convicted prisoners in the Californian Department of Corrections, who are serving sentences for child molestation or rape. The authors have defined their sample clearly, in terms of inclusions and exclusions:

1. gang offences excluded
2. biological children as victims (incest) excluded.

Prisoners must:

1. be within 14–30 months of release
2. be aged between 18 and 60
3. have two or less prior felony convictions
4. admit committing their offences
5. have no ongoing criminal/legal procedings
6. have an estimated IQ of 80 or above (average)
7. speak English
8. not have a severe mental illness
9. not require skilled nursing care for medical ailments
10. not have presented severe management problems in prison.

The experimental design of the project is exemplary, and treatment effectiveness is evaluated by comparing three groups of subjects:

1. Treatment group: sex offenders who volunteer for the programme and are randomly selected for treatment.
2. Voluntary control group: sex offenders who volunteer but are not randomly selected for treatment; they are matched to the treatment subjects on the basis of age (+/− 40), type of offence (child molestation/rape and sex of victim), and criminal history.
3. Non-voluntary control group: sex offenders who qualify for the programme but chose not to participate, and matched as above.

Furthermore, the treatment programme is described in some detail, and includes:

1. a core relapse prevention group for 4.5 hours/week for 2 years
2. individual therapy for 1 hour/week
3. nursing input 2 hours/week
4. a variety of related groups
5. behavioural reconditioning provided for subjects with deviant sexual arousal patterns who give additional consent
6. year aftercare programme upon release.

The project used multiple data sources for determining reoffence rates, including official records and self-report, and decided to record re-arrests for new sexual and new violent offences separately. They took into account the attrition rate, and analysed the data both in terms of "treatment as assigned" and "treatment as delivered". Drop-outs were defined as those subjects who withdrew from the programme within at least the first year.

The findings can only be considered to be preliminary at this stage, but the authors have reported that treatment subjects were less likely to commit new sex offences than were non-volunteers; treated child molesters were less likely to commit other violent crimes than were molesters in the volunteer control group; and perhaps most importantly, a markedly high risk of reoffence was found for the small treatment drop-out group. The authors point out that this latter group comprises probably the most impulsive sex offenders, least able to exercise self-control, and yet most in need of treatment.

STEP Project (Beckett et al., 1994)

The STEP Project is important, primarily because it represents the first substantial attempt in Britain to describe and evaluate representative community-based sex offender treatment programmes run by the Probation Service.

The authors were involved in evaluating six well-established probation programmes, plus the only residential private specialist centre for the treatment of child abusers in the UK. Approximately seven men from each centre (and 20 from the residential centre) completed pre- and post-treatment measures on a range of estabished psychological tests, and received an average of 54 hours in therapy (and 462 hours treatment for the subjects in residential treatment). Two of the programmes were rolling long-term, three were short-term intensive groups, one was short-term intensive plus a co-working component; all utilised similar cognitive–behavioural techniques.

The strengths of the project lie in the careful elaboration of the content of therapy, the attempt to identify what aspects of programmes might be the most effective in producing change, the full description of the sample, and the clear aim to link the choice of evaluative measures with the aims of treatment.

Inevitably, there were methodological flaws, the most predominant of which was the absence of any form of control group, and the small number of subjects treated in each centre; the sampling method involved voluntary participation in the research study—approximately half of those approached refused to participate, 12% refused to be tested at follow-up, and 10% dropped out.

The authors concluded that successful group programmes demonstrated high levels of group cohesiveness and task orientation, there were clear structures and explicit rules, and an atmosphere was established where members felt encouraged and respected as individuals. The psychological measures, administered pre- and post-treatment demonstrated that short-term therapy had no success with highly deviant men although 54% of the sample showed a treatment effect (including some subjects who "deteriorated" on particular measures). The authors highlight the apparently inadequate cover of relapse prevention training, the failure of probation to establish systematic assessments of clients to monitor progress through treatment, and recommend the establishment of a small number of specialised residential programmes for highly deviant sex offenders.

Clearly the findings of the STEP Project can only be considered to be preliminary, and the authors point to the need for follow-up at 2, 5, and 10 years post-treatment. Only then will it be possible to explore the link between treatment centre, offender characteristics, therapeutic change as measured by psychological tests, and recidivism rates.

Challenge Project (Craissati & McClurg, 1996, 1997)

The Challenge Project—an assessment and treatment programme for perpetrators of child sexual abuse in southeast London—assessed all 80 offenders coming before the courts and the parole board over a two year period, and followed them up one and two years later. The strengths of the evaluation design lay in the sampling procedure (all convicted men within a clearly defined geographical area), and the attempt to circumvent the ethical difficulties of a control group by comparing the efficacy of clearly articulated group and individual methods of treatment (see Fig. 7.1 for referral process).

The subjects were interviewed and a number of standardised tests administered, which were repeated one year later. Subjects who were considered appropriate and were available for community treatment were selected for either group or individual treatment, matched on extremes of IQ (>100 and <75) and age (>60 and <25), a history of sexual/violent convictions, and gender of the victim. A third, "miscellaneous", group was made up of men who were unable to participate in the treatment programme, mainly because recommendations for community treatment were not followed by the courts or parole board. The cognitive– behavioural treatment programme for the group and individual treatment conditions was identical, and was detailed—session by session—in a manual available for all the therapists, all of whom had a similar level of counselling

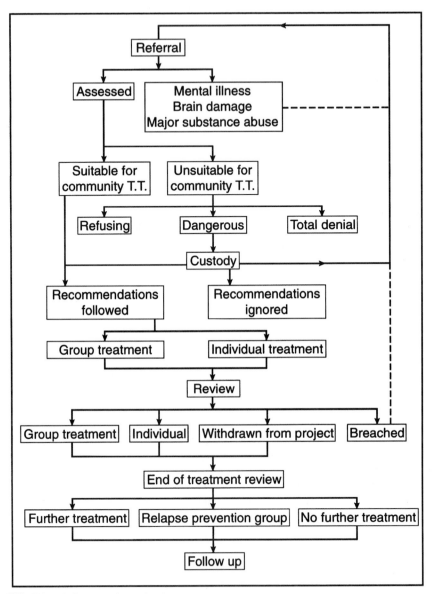

FIG. 7.1   Challenge Project referral process.

skills and knowledge of working with sexual offenders, and all of whom received supervision from a senior probation officer and clinical psychologist. Follow-up comprised official records, self-report and unofficial agency reports. Although the miscellaneous group were included, clearly they did not represent a control condition as they comprised some of the most serious and risky offenders.

Although test scores were available at the point of assessment, a significant number of men refused to complete questionnaires one year later, which made statistical analysis more difficult, and a cautious conclusion was reached in favour of group treatment. At this preliminary stage of follow-up, the authors were interested to investigate the importance of compliance (versus non-compliance) in the treatment programme as a possible predictor of recidivism: non-compliers were defined as those subjects who were reconvicted of any further offence during or following treatment, or were breached for any reason during the course of treatment, or did not complete the programme for any reason (e.g. dropping out after status became informal/voluntary, failing to comply with a condition of treatment, or removal for mental health reasons), or were poor attenders missing more than two sessions during the programme. A logistic regression analysis revealed that non-compliers were significantly more likely to have had a previous sexual or violent conviction, and to have had a history of childhood sexual victimisation.

At the two-year follow-up, 8 of the 43 men treated on the project were considered to be "project failures". However, only one had been reconvicted for a sexual offence—possession of child pornography—which occurred at the beginning of his community sentence. One further man was reconvicted of violence towards his adult female partner. Almost all of the "project failures" (88%) had offended against acquaintances or strangers; all but one had themselves been sexually abused as children; most had previous convictions for violent or sexual offences. The authors are quite clear that follow-up needs to be extended to 5 and 10 years, and that non-compliers and those lost to follow-up must be taken into account when investigating recidivism rates.

CASE STUDIES

At the two-year follow-up, **Kevin**—who had entered the group treatment programme—completed the post-treatment questionnaires, and was again seen one year further on. On tests, he appeared to have improved Hostility and Fear of Negative Evaluation scores, levels of psychological denial and cognitive distortions were reduced, and he showed more honesty in reporting paedophilic-type characteristics. Eventually he entered a new relationship (without children in the home) and found new employment.

Tom's period of parole ended nine months after he entered group treatment. He always contributed to therapy spontaneously and appeared to be highly compliant; however, although he continued to attend on a voluntary basis for six weeks, he dropped out after the Easter break, during which time he knew his ex-wife was remarrying (and was thus rated as "non-compliant"). He thwarted all attempts to contact him and offer support, and only resumed any form of contact when he was reconvicted, two years later, of grievous bodily harm against his new partner, having dealt her a single but serious blow to the face; their relationship had apparently been characterised by increasing levels of jealousy on his part.

Peter was clearly one of the treatment programme "non-compliers": he was discharged from the group after missing one session, warnings for lateness, and behaving aggressively to the therapists when under the influence of alcohol. When taken back to court for breach of his condition of treatment, he was re-sentenced to custody for one year. Although he refused to complete research questionnaires upon his release, information was available one year later which suggested that although he continued to present a cause for concern, he had not been arrested for any further offences, sexual or otherwise.

George completed post-treatment questionnaires and demonstrated improved Fear of Negative Evaluation and lower levels of Hostility. Other scores demonstrated little change because they were initially very low; these included his understanding of the need for treatment, cognitive distortions and paedophilic traits. He had developed a good relapse prevention plan and was continually self-monitoring. At follow-up he was married with two children of his own; he reported fleeting sexualised thoughts towards boys half a dozen times a year, which he understood as being triggered by transient anxieties or insecurities in his relationship. There was no evidence— formal or informal—to suggest that he had reoffended.

The case studies were chosen to demonstrate some of the key issues in the assessment and treatment of perpetrators of child sexual abuse, and therefore are not representative of the vast majority of perpetrators passing through the Challenge Project treatment programme, most of whom are at least superficially compliant and have not been rearrested at follow-up. If their progress is viewed more informally, then a few further comments can be made.

It would seem that Kevin's engagement in treatment could equally have resulted in greater defensiveness and entrenched attitudes in an attempt to salvage some remnants of fragile self-esteem; employing motivational interviewing techniques appeared to be instrumental in avoiding such a situation, and his relatively low levels of psychological disturbance allowed for maximum change within a group setting.

Tom, however, was extremely badly damaged by his childhood victimisation experiences, sexual and otherwise, and had recourse to no other "nurturing" relationship. His apparent engagement in treatment was confused with his ability to elicit the profound concern and empathy of therapists and group members alike, and with time it became clear that he was in no way able to come to terms with his past. Although in many ways, he exerted considerable self-control in his life, it was only in his intimate relationships that he acted out his intrapsychic conflicts. Although the risk of him reoffending against a child remains very unclear, it may be that he would need to engage in dynamic psychotherapy on an individual basis in order to address his broad-ranging difficulties.

Peter, of course, must remain high risk, and there is little to suggest that an individual or a psychodynamic approach would have fared better. Whether or not he chose to assimilate any of the cognitive–behavioural concepts remains unclear. Any future reoffence is likely to result in a life sentence, and antilibidinal medication might need to be considered if he were willing to comply.

George represents an all too small subgroup of perpetrators whose ability to view their offending with clear eyes emerges some time after their arrest and during incarceration; there is little doubt that although he would have been an asset to the group treatment programme, it would have been wasted time; a combination of developing emotional insight and a relapse prevention plan appear to have provided him with a level of real psychological change. In internalising the therapist in a positive way, he may have sufficient strength to carry him through, although the situation will inevitably remain precarious at times of stress. He knows he has open access to the clinic, and such an offer of support may be crucial in these rather dependent perpetrators.

Summary of case studies

The four cases are all based on clients who have been referred to the Challenge Project over the past four years. Names have been changed, as well as certain details in the background history and offending behaviour, in order to preserve confidentiality. The stories are representative of the bulk of perpetrators referred to the project.

TOM (AGED 38)

Tom was referred at the point of parole. He had been convicted of three counts of indecent assault on his daughter, Mary, over a five year period when she was aged 8–13. He received a six year sentence, and was granted parole with a condition to attend group treatment in the community. His period of parole ended three months before the end of treatment.

Tom presented with little denial for the actual convictions, and agreed that they were specimen charges. He viewed himself with disgust, and was clear that Mary's life was irrevocably altered by his behaviour. He fully acknowledged the degree of aggression involved, and the fact that Mary colluded out of fear, not enjoyment. He did not have intercourse with her, because the abuse was not about sexual attraction. His anger was directed towards his ex-wife, who he viewed as unfaithful, believing that Mary was not his child, but that of his wife's lover. He never confronted her with this belief, but married the dates of the affair with conception. The abuse occurred once his wife left the household (and the children) and Tom had custody for a while. The abuse continued once Mary was again living with her mother, and visiting (whilst Tom retained custody of his son). No abuse of the son was suspected, but there were difficulties in demonstrating physical affection with him, and feelings of jealousy at the care and attention he bestowed upon him. The abuse was characterised by feelings of wanting "to take back what had been taken from me".

Tom's background was characterised by profound emotional, physical, and sexual abuse at the hands of his step-father. He could understand that his mother was disabled, but still he had resented her withdrawal and lack of protection. He perceived sexual abuse at the time as being preferable to a beating/humiliation. He was bullied at school, but then learnt to retaliate; drugs and alcohol were part of his life when he left school, and he was involved in some street violence, but subsequently settled for 10 years with turbulence mainly manifesting itself in two heterosexual relationships. He felt he sought out women who might let him down, felt used, then justified his anger towards them, occasionally resorting to physical violence. Close questioning revealed adult homosexual contacts occasionally, and coercive sexual practices with his girlfriends, involving a degree of humiliation.

Tom was assessed as posing a low/medium risk of sexual reoffending—the offences had contained considerable overt aggression and he clearly had relationship problems—but violent reoffending appeared to be more likely, given the pervasive use of violence in all relationships and an earlier history of antisocial behaviour.

Tom was considered appropriate for group treatment (cognitive–behavioural) because this would provide the opportunity to develop warm and supportive relationships with the other group members, in contrast to his confrontational macho style in the outside world. The intensity of his relationship with his profoundly abusive father mitigated against individual treatment, where the transference was likely to be overwhelming in terms of his fear of dependency and need to rebel against threatening intimacy. Relatively low levels of denial meant that he could help other group members face up to their own distortions, whereas he would find other aspects of the programme emotionally challenging.

Progress in therapy was coloured by Tom's irritation at the other men not being honest. He would castigate himself to the point where leaders were concerned about his wellbeing, and they would refrain from pushing him on areas he found difficult. His apparent honesty was contrasted by his rather seductive references to "things my dad did"; he was a powerful member of the group who controlled by a quiet menace or by the dreadful frankness about his offences or own victim experiences which silenced the others. He continued to attend after his parole ended for some weeks, but dropped out after the Easter break, during which time his ex-wife remarried (and he was thus rated as 'non-compliant'). He thwarted all attempts to contact him and offer support, and only resumed any form of contact when he was reconvicted—two years later—of grievous bodily harm against his new partner, having dealt her a single but serious blow to the face; their relationship had apparently been characterised by increasing levels of jealousy on his part. Given the profoundly destructive nature of Tom's early life experiences, and the broad nature of his psychopathology, it is not clear whether a sex offender group is necessarily the treatment of choice.

PETER (AGED 48)

Peter was referred for treatment at the point of sentencing. He was convicted of one charge of indecent assault on a 5-year-old girl who lived down his road. He allegedly put his hand down her underpants and touched her vagina, subsequent to which she told her mother. In his 20s, he received convictions first for rape, then buggery, on pre-pubescent girls, for which he received substantial prison sentences. Ten years later, he was convicted for indecent assault. He subsequently stopped drinking alcohol, which had been grossly implicated in his offending behaviour. He had married a woman who herself was very vulnerable—of low intelligence and abused—and had a daughter who denied that he had ever interfered with her. Given the relatively minor nature of his index offence, he was given a probation order with a condition to attend group treatment.

Peter denied that he touched the girl (Rosie) under her pants, but acknowledged that he had engaged in horseplay with her, and that he had thought about her in a sexual way that day. He blamed the authorities for never offering him help, acknowledging that his sexual attraction for young girls got him into trouble. He discussed his sexual interests openly, and wanted treatment so that he could avoid any further trouble, although prison posed no threat. It was probable that he wanted to persuade social services to allow family rehabilitation. He said he had had one alcoholic drink prior to the offence.

Peter's background details were vague. He appeared to have distant parents who worked hard and failed to set boundaries for his behaviour, and he was mainly in the company of other boys. He reported one incident of sexual abuse in the park when a drunken woman forced him to perform oral sex on her. He denied any feelings around this incident of fear, disgust, or enjoyment, only annoyance that his peers abandoned him. He later made friends with an older boy of 19 who encouraged him to talk about sexual fantasies of girls at the swimming pool. He had numerous early convictions for theft, as well as the sexual offences, although these reduced in frequency over time. He had worked in a number of casual, unskilled jobs, although he was of average intelligence, and socially skilled.

Peter was assessed as posing a high risk of sexual reoffending, despite the relatively minor nature of his index offence. He clearly articulated a persistent deviant sexual interest (not laboratory tested), he had a number of prior sexual convictions involving violence and penetration and commencing at a young age, he had been dependent on alcohol for many years, and had an earlier history of antisocial behaviour. Externally driven motivation to abstain from reoffending was fuelled by his knowledge that future reconviction would result in an extremely long prison sentence.

Peter was placed in the group (cognitive–behavioural) essentially because the court wished it, and we were concerned to try treatment as an alternative to a very brief custodial sentence. The high levels of sexual deviancy and antisocial behaviour in the past posed a problem to both group or individual work. It was felt that the group might be able to contain some of the perverse dynamics which would erupt in individual work in terms of a battle for control. The therapists anticipated a battle of sorts regarding boundaries—time keeping, completing homework and alcohol.

Peter's behaviour in therapy was coloured by his need to take control, and thereby sabotage any threat of intimacy. He was occasionally late, and smelt of alcohol. He encouraged talk of fantasies, and reverted to sexualised discussion whenever asked about his feelings. The therapists became more adept at ignoring sexual comments and always drawing him out on feelings, moving away from encouraging explicit descriptions of offending. After missing one session for transport disruptions, warnings for lateness, and behaving aggressively to the leaders when under the influence of alcohol, he was taken back to court and breached, receiving a one year custodial sentence. Although he refused to complete research questionnaires upon his release, information was available one year later which suggested that although he continued to present a cause for concern, he had not been arrested for any further offences, sexual or otherwise. Whether or not he chose to assimilate any of the cognitive–behavioural concepts remains unclear, and any future reoffence is likely to result in a life sentence.

GEORGE (AGED 22)

George was convicted of two specimen charges of indecent assault on his step-nephew, John, between the ages of 7–12. He made a serious suicide attempt following his cathartic confession to the police, and subsequently served a five year prison sentence. Although he did not seek help at the time, he began to question his behaviour during his period of incarceration. He formed one brief adult homosexual relationship upon his release, prior to moving in with, and subsequently marrying a woman. It was on a voluntary basis that he sought treatment, as he viewed his offending behaviour now as abhorrent, and was fearful of reoffending.

George made no attempt to minimise the extent of the offending behaviour, and had already begun to face up to the shallow and selfish nature of his "love". He felt loved in his current relationship, and sexually satisfied finally. However, he occasionally found himself looking at boys in the street with unformed sexual urges, none of which he carried out. These thoughts made him extremely anxious, and he made attempts not to be alone with boys.

George's background was one of emotional deprivation: his mother left when he was eight because, he later gathered, of her interest in other men, and his father was a heavy drinker, bad tempered but not violent. The predominant feature of childhood was his seduction into a child pornography ring, with other boys. This provided him with a form of loving which was absent at home, sexual companionship with another, much loved, boy, and a form of parenting. He did not view these experiences as abuse, although he did not like the aggressive style of the female abuser in the family. The contact ceased abruptly when he was 13 (the family disappeared) and there was no further sexual contact until he met, and seduced his victim, John. Throughout adult life, he held down steady skilled employment, and had no drink, drug or forensic history.

George was assessed as posing a moderate risk of sexual reoffending: his victim was male, and his sexual interest in boys commenced at a very young age; he also had relationship problems which had only recently improved. The risk was perhaps mitigated by his clear distaste for his offending behaviour and his terror of losing his new family.

George was placed in individual therapy, with a focus on psychodynamic processes linking his own early sexual victimisation with his unconscious motives for offending. His very low levels of denial rendered the cognitive–behavioural approach largely redundant, and the utter deprivation he suffered in childhood suggested that he needed the experience of a consistent, boundaried and attentive therapist on whom he could develop a healthy level of dependency.

George entered individual therapy for one year, followed by monthly follow-up for one year. He was fully committed and became quite dependent on the therapist who took on the role of the mother he never had. Themes in therapy were mourning the loss of the idea of a loving relationship, gradually accepting the reality of the abuse. George was much more comfortable discussing the offence—appropriately—than recalling his unhappy family life or the pornography ring. Acknowledging his own experience of being buggered in a session immediately resulted in a strong desire to seek comfort by masturbating a boy, as he left the session. The theme of grieving was continued as he relinquished the idealised substitute family of his childhood, and acknowledged some of his anger at being used and physically hurt, particularly his need for his mother—previously denied—and anger towards women.

At follow-up, George had developed a good relapse prevention plan and was continually self-monitoring. He had completed post-treatment questionnaires and demonstrated improved Fear of Negative Evaluation scores and lower levels of Hostility. Other scores demonstrated little change because they were initially very low. He was married with two children of his own; he reported fleeting sexualised thoughts towards boys half a dozen times a year, which he understood as being triggered by transient anxieties or insecurities in his relationship. There was no evidence—formal or informal—to suggest that he had reoffended. In internalising the therapist in a positive way, he may have sufficient strength to carry him through, although the situation will inevitably remain precarious at times of stress.

KEVIN (AGED 35)

Kevin was referred for treatment at the point of sentencing. He was charged with the indecent assault of his 12-year-old step-daughter, Sally, over a four month period. He received a probation order with a condition to attend group treatment.

Kevin acknowledged that he had engaged in fondling Sally, asking her to masturbate him and lie on top of him and kissing her on the mouth. He vehemently denied her allegations of digital penetration and attempted intercourse, saying that he was "not a pervert". He knew, as the adult, he should have taken responsibility, but felt himself to be helpless in the face of her "sexual precociousness and seductiveness". He was preoccupied with the way he had been treated by Sally's grandmother who he described as "an interfering old witch", and who had forced his partner to choose between him and her. Motivation for treatment was predominantly related to a terror of prison, and some superficial acknowledgement that he "should have said no".

Kevin's background was discontented but not unduly disturbed. His mother was an attractive woman, apparently concerned with her appearance, who called him the "man of the family". His father was in the Army, and did not live with them, visiting perhaps twice during his childhood. On these occasions, he was locked out of the house whilst his parents apparently made love. He was a shy child, embarrassed about his lack of father, and bullied at school. He truanted occasionally, but never retaliated. He lacked confidence in relationships, and after a few rejections by women, he tended not to embark on relationships. However, he met Sally's mother prior to the offences when he came to her rescue, fighting off her violent boyfriend. He had no drug, alcohol, or forensic history.

Kevin was assessed as posing a low risk of sexual reoffending as he presented with only relationship problems as a negative predictive factor. The threat of prison was a considerable additional deterrent.

Kevin was considered to be ideally suited to the cognitive–behavioural group approach because of the nature of his denial. His distorted perceptions were readily apparent but not overly fixed, many of them were held on to in an attempt to preserve some self-esteem. It was felt that he might accept challenges from his peers more readily than from a potential individual female therapist who could provoke many of his ambivalent feelings towards his mother.

Despite considerable denial, Kevin settled well into group treatment. If directly challenged, he reverted to a stance of denial, but he participated in an active and interested fashion. He learnt to talk about his feelings of inadequacy, and the element of anger and revenge in his offending behaviour. He appeared to benefit from the sharing of anecdotes, and general supportive attention. At follow-up he had entered a new relationship, found new employment, and was able to talk appropriately about his offending and his motivations.

At the two-year follow-up, Keven completed the post-treatment questionnaires. On tests, he appeared to have improved Hostility and Fear of Negative

Evaluation scores, levels of psychological denial and cognitive distortions were reduced, and he showed more honesty in reporting paedophilic-type characteristics. Utilising motivational interviewing techniques appeared to be instrumental in avoiding greater defensiveness and entrenched attitudes, and Kevin's relatively low levels of psychological disturbance allowed for maximum change within a group setting.

Eventually he entered a new relationship (without children in the home) and found new employment.

Rating scales

MULTIPHASIC SEX INVENTORY
(NICHOLS & MOLINDER, 1984)

This 300 item questionnaire produces 20 clinical scales and a sexual history. The scales have been standardised on sex offender and college control samples, including untreated and treated comparisons where appropriate. Norms are available from the authors. Respondents are asked to mark their answers on the answer sheet, True (T) or False (F); a taped version is available for those clients with literacy problems. Samples of questions are outlined below.

Child molest scale

"The CM scale is designed to measure the type of offender (paedophile) who manipulates and coerces a victim(s) to comply with his demands."

• Sometimes I am sexually attracted to children
• It would peak my interest to learn that a child is curious about sex
• People have commented about my love for children

Rape scale

"The type of sex offender that the R Scale identifies is the 'blitz' type sex offender (rapist). He may strike without warning and always frightens the victim."

- The thought of overpowering someone sexually has been stimulating to me
- I have had to fight the impulse to rape
- I have been accused of purposely hurting someone in a sexual encounter

Exhibitionism scale

- It would interest me to learn that a female would want me to expose to her
- I have often looked for someone to expose to
- I have been so excited while exposing that I have reached out and grabbed hold of a person (answer only if you have exposed yourself)

Paraphilias: Atypical Sexual Outlet Subtest

1. Fetish scale
2. Obscene call scale
3. Voyeurism scale
4. Bondage & discipline scale
5. Sado-masochism scale

A critical item list of eight items taken from the five scale should act as a "stop-sign" to the tester should any of these items be endorsed.

- I have reached orgasm while secretly watching some
- I have beaten a person during a sexual encounter
- I have fantasized about killing someone during sex

Sexual Dysfunction Subtest

1. Sexual inadequacies scale
2. Premature ejaculation scale
3. Physical disabilities scale
4. Impotence scale

"The SI scale has the single purpose of identifying the sex offender who feels socially inadequate ... The PE scale ... is a straightforward assessment of an offender's perception of himself regarding his sexual functioning. ... The PD scale ... address sexual dysfunction from a physical disability standpoint ... The Im scale is a measure of a client's helplessness and possible hopelessness." The endorsement of any of the critical eight items list indicates that the assessor should evaluate further.

- I believe there is something wrong with my sex organs
- Most of the time I cannot get an erection when I would like to have sex
- I am very sad and blue and I am not interested in sex

Sex knowledge and beliefs scale

"The items relate only to sexual anatomy and physiology, and not to the reproductive systems."

- The glans of the clitoris is generally about the size of a pea
- To have a sex orgasm means the same as to have a climax
- During sexual intercourse, the penis can get caught in the vagina

Validity Subtest

(a) Parallel items scale

The PI scale consists of items from the Multiphasic Sex Inventory that match items from the MMPI.

(b) Social sexual desirability scale

"The SSD was designed to measure "normal" sexual interest and drive, and to help identify persons who are responding to the Multiphasic Sex Inventory is a socially desirable response set."

- It would interest me to learn that a female has felt pleasure from masturbating herself

(c) Sexual obsessions scale

"The SO scale has two purposes: to measure a person's tendencies to exaggerate his problem and to assess the individual's obsession with sex."

- I regularly have had several orgasms in one day

(d) Lie scales

Accountability scales

(a) Cognitive distortion and immaturity scale

"The CDI scale is intended to assess early childhood cognitive distortions which stay with the offender and help him to set the stage for his personality disorder and potential to act out sexually deviant impulses. It is specifically designed to measure the victim stance."

- I do not believe I have had to overcome more in life than most people

(b) Justifications scale

"The Ju scale's sole purpose is to measure the degree the sex offender attempts to justify his sexually deviant behaviour."

- My sex offence would not have occurred if I had not become interested in the child's sexual growth and development (answer only if you have had sexual contact with a child)

(c) Treatment attitudes scale

"The TA scale . . . is an expression of an individual's attitude regarding his openness for treatment."

- Even without any treatment I know that I can control my sexual behaviour

Sex history

"The sex history is divided into five sections, namely:

1. Sex Deviance Development
2. Marriage Development
3. Gender Orientation Development
4. Gender Identity Development
5. Sexual Assault Behaviour"

- I suspect my father forced himself sexually on my mother
- I have had one or more affairs while married
- I am privately attracted to members of my own sex

Permission to use sample items from the Multiphasic Sex Inventory has been granted by the authors, H.R. Nichols & I. Molinder, 437 Bowes Drive, Tacoma, WA 98466–7047 USA.

A MULTIDIMENSIONAL APPROACH TO INDIVIDUAL DIFFERENCES IN EMPATHY (DAVIS, 1980)

This 28 item scale rates respondents' capacity for general empathy, and contains items related to both cognitive role-taking and emotional responsiveness. Respondents are asked to answer each item on a 5-point scale running from 0 (does not describe me well), to 4 (describes me very well). The four 7 item subscales are described as follows (with the mean scores for male college controls in brackets):

(a) Perspective-taking.   This assesses spontaneous attempts to adopt the perspectives of other people and see things from their points of view (16.78).

(b) Fantasy.   This measures the tendency to identify with characters in movies, novels, plays and other fictional situations (15.73).

(c) Empathic concern.   This inquires about respondents' feelings of warmth, compassion, and concern for others (19.04).

(d) Personal distress.   This measures the personal feelings of anxiety and discomfort that result from observing another's negative experience (9.46).

Sample items:

1. I daydream and fantasise with some regularity about things that might happen to me.(f)
2. I often have tender, concerned feelings for people less fortunate than me.(ec)
6. In emergency situations, I feel apprehensive and ill-at-ease.(pd)
11. I sometimes try to understand my friends better by imagining how things look from their perspective.(pt)
12. Becoming extremely involved in a good book or movie is somewhat rare for me.(f)
15. If I'm sure I'm right about something, I don't waste much time listening to other people's arguments.(pt)
20. I am often quite touched by things that I see happen.(ec)
27. When I see someone who badly needs help in an emergency, I go to pieces.(pd)

Source: *A Multidimensional Approach to Individual Differences in Empathy*, Davis, M.H. (1980). Copyright (c) 1980, Select Press. Sample items reprinted with permission. The complete scale and manual is available from Select Press, Box 37, Corte Madera, CA 94 976, USA; tel: 415/435–4461; SelectPr@aol. com

ATTITUDES TOWARDS WOMEN (SPENCE & HELMREICH, 1978, 1972)

This 25 item scale rates respondents' views towards various aspects of women's role—vocational, educational, intellectual, and interpersonal relationships. Respondents are asked to answer each statement on a 4-point scale from "agree strongly" to "disagree strongly", and the items are scored from 0 to 3. Three indicates a more egalitarian or liberal attitude towards women, whereas 0 indicates a more conservative or traditionally patriarchal attitude. Thus items

1,4,5,10,13,14,15,16,17,19,20, and 22 should be scored with A ("agree strongly") scoring 0 and D ("disagree strongly") scoring 3; the remaining items are scored in reverse. The possible total scores range from 0 to 75. Scores can be expected to differ by social class; Hogue (1991), and Craissati and McClurg (1996) found untreated sex offenders to score an average of 54 and 53 respectively.

1. Swearing and obscenity are more repulsive in the speech of a woman than of a man.
2. Women should take increasing responsibility for leadership in solving the intellectual and social problems of the day.
3. Both husband and wife should be allowed the same grounds of divorce.
4. Telling dirty jokes should be mostly a masculine prerogative.
5. Intoxication among women is worse than intoxication among men.
6. Under modern economic conditions with women being active outside the home, men should share in household tasks such as washing dishes and doing the laundry.
7. It is insulting to women to have the "obey" clause remain in the marriage service.
8. There should be a strict merit system in job appointment and promotion without regard to sex.
9. A woman should be as free as a man to propose marriage.
10. Women should worry less about their rights and more about becoming good wives and mothers.
11. Women earning as much as their dates should bear equally the expense when they go out together.
12. Women should assume their rightful place in business and all the professions along with men.
13. A woman should not expect to go to exactly the same places or to have quite the same freedom of action as a man.
14. Sons in a family should be given more encouragement to go to college than daughters.
15. It is ridiculous for a woman to run a locomotive and for a man to darn socks.
16. In general, the father should have greater authority than the mother in the bringing up of children.
17. Women should be encouraged not to become sexually intimate with anyone before marriage even their fiances.
18. The husband should not be favoured by law over the wife in the disposal of family property or income.
19. Women should be concerned with their duties of childbearing and house tending, rather than with desires for professional and business careers.
20. The intellectual leadership of a community should be largely in the hands of men.

21. Economics and social freedom is worth far more to women than acceptance of the ideal of femininity which has been set up by men.
22. On the average, women should be regarded as less capable of contributing to economic production than are men.
23. There are many jobs in which men should be given preference over women in being hired or promoted.
24. Women should be given equal opportunity with men for apprenticeships in the various trades.
25. The modern girl is entitled to the same freedom from regulation and control that is given to the modern boy.

Source: *From Masculinity and femininity: Their psychological dimensions, correlates, and antecedents.* J.T. Spence & R.L. Helmreich. Copyright (c) 1978. With permission of the University of Texas Press.

FEAR OF NEGATIVE EVALUATION SCALE (WATSON & FRIEND, 1969)

This 30 item scale rates respondents' sensitivity to negative evaluations by others, expectations, and avoidance of criticism. Respondents are asked to rate each statement as true or false, as it pertains to them, and one point is given for each answer that matches the scoring key: true (2,3,5,7,9,11,13,14,17,19,20,22,24,25,28,29,30); and false (1,4,6,8,10,12,15,16,18,21,23,26,27). Low scorers fall between 0 and 8; average scorers between 9 and 18; and high scorers (sensitive to possible criticism) fall between 19 and 30. Previous studies of sexual offenders found average untreated scores to be 18.6 (Craissati & McClurg, 1996) and 16.4 (Hopkins, 1991). Interestingly, Craissati & McClurg (1997) found that those subjects who refused to re-complete the psychometric tests one year later, scored significantly higher than the compliant subjects on the Fear of Negative Evaluation Scale at the assessment stage.

1. I rarely worry about seeming foolish to others.
2. I worry about what people will think of me even when I know it doesn't make any difference.
3. I become tense and jittery if I know someone is sizing me up.
4. I am unconcerned even if I know people are forming an unfavourable impression of me.
5. I feel very upset when I commit some social error.
6. The opinions that important people have of me cause me little concern.
7. I am often afraid that I may look ridiculous or make a fool of myself.
8. I react very little when other people disapprove of me.
9. I am frequently afraid of other people noticing my shortcomings.

10. The disapproval of others would have little effect on me.
11. If someone is evaluating me, I tend to expect the worst.
12. I rarely worry about what kind of impression I am making on someone.
13. I am afraid that others will not approve of me.
14. I am afraid that people will find fault with me.
15. Other people's opinions of me do not bother me.
16. I am not necessarily upset if I do not please someone.
17. When I am talking to someone, I worry about what they may be thinking of me.
18. I feel that you can't help making social errors sometimes, so why worry about it.
19. I am usually worried about what kind of impression I make.
20. I worry a lot about what my superiors think of me.
21. If I know someone is judging me, it has little effect on me.
22. I worry that others will think I am not worthwhile.
23. I worry very little about what others may think of me.
24. Sometimes I think I am too concerned with what other people think of me.
25. I often worry that I will say or do the wrong things.
26. I am often indifferent to the opinions others have of me.
27. I am usually confident that others will have a favourable impression of me.
28. I often worry that people who are important to me won't think very much of me.
29. I brood about the opinions my friends have about me.
30. I become tense and jittery if I know I am being judged by my superiors.

Source: Watson, D. & Friend, R. (1969). Measurement of social evaluative-anxiety. *Journal of Consulting and Clinical Psychology, 33*, 448–457. Copyright (c) 1969, American Psychological Association. Reprinted with permission of the publisher and the author.

BUSS–DURKEE HOSTILITY INVENTORY (BUSS & DURKEE, 1957)

This 66 item scale rates respondents' general anger and hostility. It can be broken down into seven subscales: negativism, resentment, indirect hostility, assault, suspicion, irritability and verbal hostility. Respondents are asked to rate each statement as true or false, as it pertains to them, and one point is assigned for every answer that matches the following scoring key:

Negativism: true (1,8,15,22,29)
Resentment: true (2,9.16,23,30,42,48); false (36)
Indirect hostility: true (3,16,31,37,49,54); false (10,24,43)
Assault: true (4,18,25,32,44,50,55,59); false (11,38)
Suspicion: true (5,12,19,26,33,39,45,51); false (56,60)

Irritability: true (6,20,27,40,46,52,57,63); false (13,34,61)
Verbal hostility: true (7,14,21,28,41,47,53,62,64); false (35,58,65,66)

The average scores (plus standard deviations) obtained from college students in the original study were: negativism (2.19, s.d. 1.34); resentment (2.26, s.d. 1.89); indirect hostility (4.47, s.d. 2.23); assault (5.07, s.d. 2.48); suspicion (3.33, s.d. 2.07); verbal hostility (7.61, s.d. 2.74); irritability (5.94, s.d. 2.65); and a total average score of 30.87 (s.d. 10.24). Craissati and McClurg (1996) found identical total average scores on their sample of untreated child sex offenders.

1. Unless somebody asks me in a nice way, I won't do what they want.
2. I don't seem to get what's coming to me.
3. I sometimes spread gossip about people I don't like.
4. Once in a while I cannot control my urge to harm others.
5. I know that people tend to talk about me behind my back.
6. I lose my temper easily but get over it quickly.
7. When I disapprove of my friend's behaviour, I let them know it.
8. When someone makes a rule I don't like, I am tempted to break it.
9. Other people always seem to get the breaks.
10. I never get mad enough to throw things.
11. I can think of no good reason for ever hitting anyone.
12. I tend to be on my guard with people who are somewhat more friendly than I expected.
13. I am always patient with others.
14. I often find myself disagreeing with people.
15. When someone is bossy, I do the opposite of what he asks.
16. When I look back on what's happened to me, I can't help feeling mildly resentful.
17. When I am mad, I sometimes slam doors.
18. If somebody hits me first, I let him have it.
19. There are a number of people who seem to dislike me very much.
20. I am irritated a great deal more than people are aware of.
21. I can't help getting into arguments with people when they disagree with me.
22. When people are bossy, I take my time just to show them.
23. Almost every week I see someone I dislike.
24. I never play practical jokes.
25. Whoever insults me or my family is asking for a fight.
26. There are a number of people who seem to be jealous of me.
27. It makes my blood boil to have somebody make fun of me.
28. I demand that people respect my rights.
29. Occasionally when I am mad at someone I will give him the "silent treatment".
30. Although I don't show it, I am sometimes eaten up with jealousy.
31. When I am angry, I sometimes sulk.

32. People who continually pester you are asking for a punch in the nose.
33. I sometimes have the feeling that others are laughing at me.
34. If someone doesn't treat me right, I don't let it annoy me.
35. Even when my anger is aroused, I don't use "strong language".
36. I don't know any people that I downright hate.
37. I sometimes pout when I don't get my way.
38. I seldom strike back, even if someone hits me first.
39. My motto is "Never trust strangers".
40. Sometimes people bother me by just being around.
41. If somebody annoys me, I am apt to tell him what I think of him.
42. If I let people see the way I feel, I'd be considered a hard person to get along with.
43. Since the age of ten, I have never had a temper tantrum.
44. When I really lose my temper, I am capable of slapping someone.
45. I commonly wonder what hidden reason another person may have for doing something nice for me.
46. I often feel like a powder keg ready to explode.
47. When people yell at me, I yell back.
48. At times I feel I get a raw deal out of life.
49. I can remember being so angry that I picked up the nearest thing and broke it.
50. I get into fights about as often as the next person.
51. I used to think that most people told the truth but now I know otherwise.
52. I sometimes carry a chip on my shoulder.
53. When I get mad, I say nasty things.
54. I sometimes show my anger by banging on the table.
55. If I have to resort to physical violence to defend my rights, I will.
56. I have no enemies who really wish to harm me.
57. I can't help being a little rude to people I don't like.
58. I could not put someone in his place, even if he needed it.
59. I have known people who pushed me so far that we came to blows.
60. I seldom feel that people are trying to anger or insult me.
61. I don't let a lot of unimportant things irritate me.
62. I often make threats I don't really mean to carry out.
63. Lately, I have been kind of grouchy.
64. When arguing, I tend to raise my voice.
65. I generally cover up my poor opinion of others.
66. I would rather concede a point than get into an argument about it.

Source: Buss, A.H. & Durkee, A. (1957). An inventory for assessing different kinds of hostility. *Journal of Consulting Psychology, 21*, 343–349. Copyright (c) 1957, American Psychological Association. Reprinted with permission of the publisher and author.

References

Abel, G.G., Becker, J.V., & Cunningham-Rathner, J. (1984). Complications, consent and cognitions in sex between children and adults. *International Journal of Law and Psychiatry, 7*, 89–103.

Abel, G.G., Becker, J.V., Mittelman, M.S., Cunningham-Rathner, J., Rouleau, J.L., & Murphy, W.D. (1987). Self reported sex crimes of non-incarcerated paraphiliacs. *Journal of Interpersonal Violence, 2*, 3–25.

Baker, A. & Duncan, S.I. (1985). Child sexual abuse: a study of prevalence in Great Britain. *Child Abuse and Neglect, 9*, 457–467.

Barker, M. & Beech, A. (1993). Sex offender treatment programmes: a critical look at the cognitive-behavioural approach. *Issues in Criminological and Legal Psychology, 19*, 37–42.

Beck, A.T. (1976). *Cognitive therapy and the emotional disorders.* New York: International Universities Press.

Beckett, R. (1994). Assessment of sex offenders. In T. Morrison, M. Erooga, & R.C. Beckett (Eds), *Sexual offending against children—assessment and treatment of male abusers*, pp. 55–79. London: Routledge.

Beckett, R., Beech, A., Fisher, D., & Fordham, A. (1994). *Community-based treatment for sex offenders: an evaluation of seven treatment programmes.* London: HMSO.

Bentovim, A. (1988). Understanding the phenomenon of sexual abuse—a family systems view of causation. In Bentovim, A., Elton, A., Hildebrand, J., Tranter, M., & Vizard, E. (Eds), *Child sexual abuse within the family: Assessment and treatment.* Bristol, England: John Wright.

Bentovim, A. (1996). Systems theory. In C. Cordess & M. Cox (Eds) *Forensic psychotherapy.* London: Jessica Kingsley Publishers.

Briere, J. & Runtz, M. (1989). University males sexual interest in children: predicting potential indices of "paedophilia" in a nonforensic sample. *Child Abuse and Neglect, 13*, 65–75.

Buss, A.H. & Durkee, A. (1957). An inventory for assessing different kinds of hostility. *Journal of Consulting Psychology, 21*, 343–349.

Campbell, J. (Ed.) (1995). *Assessing Dangerousness—Violence by Sexual Offenders, Batterers and Child Abusers.* California: Sage.

Coltart, N. (1987). Diagnosis and assessment for suitability for psycho-analytical psychotherapy. *British Journal of Psychotherapy, 4*, 127–134.

Craissati, J. (1994). Sex offenders and the Criminal Justice System. *Justice of the Peace, 158*, 689–691.

Craissati, J. & McClurg, G. (1996). The Challenge Project: perpetrators of child sexual abuse in S.E.London. *Child Abuse and Neglect, 20*, 1067–1077.

Craissati, J. & McClurg, G. (1997). The Challenge Project: a treatment programme evaluation for perpetrators of child sexual abuse. *Child Abuse and Neglect, 21*, 637–648.

Davis, M.H. (1980). A multidimensional approach to individual differences in empathy. *JSAS Catalog of Selected Documents in Psychology, 10*, 85.

Finkelhor, D. (1984). *Child sexual abuse: New theory and research*. New York: Free Press.

Finkelhor, D. (1986). *A sourcebook on child sexual abuse*. California: Sage.

Fisher, D. & Thornton, D. (1993). Assessing risk of re-offending in sexual offenders. *Journal of Mental Health, 2*, 105–117.

Freud, A. (1936). *The ego and the mechanism of defense*. Madison: International Universities Press.

Furby, L., Weinrott, M., & Blackshaw, L. (1989). Sex offender recidivism: a review. *Psychological Bulletin, 105*, 3–30.

Furniss, T. (1991). *The multi-professional handbook of child sexual abuse. Integrated management, therapy and legal intervention*. London & New York: Routledge.

Gaddini, E. (1976). Discussion of the role of family life in child development. *International Journal of Psycho-analysis, 57*, 397–401.

George, W.H. & Marlatt, G.A. (1989). Introduction. In R.D. Laws (Ed.), *Relapse prevention with sex offenders*. New York: Guilford Press.

Glasser, M. (1979). Some aspects of the role of aggression in the perversions. In I. Rosen (Ed.), *Sexual deviation*. Oxford University Press.

Glasser, M. (1988). Psychodynamic aspects of paedophilia. *Psychoanalytic Psychotherapy, 3*, 121–135.

Glasser, M. (1990). Paedophilia. In R. Bluglass & P. Bowden (Eds), *Principles and practice of forensic psychiatry*. Edinburgh: Churchill Livingstone.

Groth, N.A., Hobson, W.F., & Gary, T.S. (1982). The child molester: clinical observations. In J. Conte & D.A. Shore (Eds), *Social work and child sexual abuse*. New York: Haworth.

Hanson, R.K. & Bussiere, M.T. (1996). *Predictors of sexual recidivism: A meta-analysis* (User Report No.1996.04). Ottowa: Dept. of the Solicitor General of Canada.

Heimann, P. (1950). On counter-transference. *International Journal of Psychoanalysis, 31*, 81–84.

Hogue, T.E. (1991). Evaluation of offence focused groups at HMP Dartmoor. *Proceedings of the Prison Psychologists' Conference*. HM Prison Service. London: HMSO.

Hollin, C.R. (1995). The meaning and implications of programme integrity. In J. McGuire (Ed.) *What works: Reducing reoffending*. Chichester: Wiley.

Hollin, C.R. & Howells, K. (1991). *Clinical approaches to sex offenders and their victims*. Chichester: Wiley.

Home Office (1988). *British Crime Survey*. London: HMSO.

Home Office (1995). *Criminal statistics England and Wales*. London: HMSO.

Home Office (1997). *Aspects of crime, children as victims*. Research & Statistics Directorate.

Hopkins, R. (1991). An evaluation of communication and social skills groups for sex offenders at HMP Frankland. *Proceedings of the Prison Psychologists' Conference*. HM Prison Service. London: HMSO.

Howells, K. (1981). Adult sexual interest in children: considerations relevant to theories of aetiology. In M. Cook & K. Howells (Eds), *Adult sexual interest in children*. London: Academic Press.

Kennedy, H.G. & Grubin, D.H. (1992). Patterns of denial in sex offenders. *Psychological Medicine, 22*, 191–196.

Knight, R.A. & Prentky, R.A. (1990). Classifying sexual offenders—the development and corroboration of taxonomic models. In W.L. Marshall, D.R. Laws & H.E. Barbaree (Eds), *Handbook of sexual assault: Issues, theories and treatment of the offender*. New York: Plenum Press.

Langevin, R. (1988). Defensiveness in sex offenders. In R. Rogers (Ed.), *Clinical assessment of malingering and deception*. New York: Guilford Press.

Laws, D.R. (Ed.) (1989). *Relapse prevention with sex offenders*. New York: Guilford Press.

Mair, K.J. (1996). Cognitive distortion in the prediction of sexual reoffending. *Issues in Criminological and Legal Psychology, 26*, 12–17.

Malan, D.H. (1979). *Individual psychotherapy and the science of psychodynamics.* London: Butterworths.

Maletzky, B.M. (1991). *Treating the sexual offender.* Newbury Park: Sage.

Mann, R. (Ed.) (1996). *Motivational interviewing with sex offenders: A practice manual.* Hull, England: NOTA Publication.

Marlatt, G.A. (1982). Relapse prevention: A self-control program for the treatment of addictive behaviors. In R.B. Stuart (Ed.), *Adherence, compliance, and generalization in behavioral medicine.* New York: Brunner/Mazel.

Marlatt, G.A. (1985). Relapse Prevention: theoretical rationale and overview of the model. In A. Marlatt & J.R. Gordon (Eds), *Relapse prevention: Maintenance strategies in the treatment of addictive behaviors.* New York: Guilford Press.

Marlatt, G.A. & Gordon, J. (1980) Determinants of relapse: implications for maintenance of change. In P.O. Davidson & S.M. Davidson (Eds) *Behavioural medicine: Changing health lifestyles.* New York: Brunner/Mazel.

Marques, J., Day, D., Nelson, C., & West, M. (1994). Effects of cognitive–behavioural treatment on sex offender recidivism. *Criminal Justice and Behaviour, 21*, 28–54.

Marshall, W.L., Jones, R., Ward, T., Johnston, P., & Barbaree, H.E. (1991). Treatment outcome with sex offenders. *Clinical Psychology Review, 11*, 465–485.

Marshall, W.L. & Pithers, W.D. (1994). A reconsideration of treatment outcome with sex offenders. *Criminal Justice and Behaviour, 21*, 10–27.

Matthews, R. (1991). Varieties of sex offender—patterns of denial. *Proceedings of the Prison Service Psychologists' Conference.* HM Prison Service. London: HMSO.

McClurg, G. & Craissati, J. (in press). Public opinion and the sentencing of perpetrators of child sexual abuse. *Journal of Sexual Aggression, 3*, 30–34.

McDougall, J. (1972). Primal scene and sexual perversion. *International Journal of Psycho-Analysis, 53*, 371.

Miller, A. (1987). *For your own good: The roots of evil in child rearing.* London: Virago Press.

Miller, W.R. (1983). Motivational interviewing with problem drinkers. *Behavioural Psychotherapy, 1*, 147–172.

Miller, W.R. & Rollnick, S. (1991). *Motivational interviewing: Preparing people to change addictive behaviour.* New York: Guilford Press.

Morrison, T., Erooga, M., & Beckett, R.C. (Eds) (1994). *Sexual offending against children—assessment and treatment of male abusers.* London: Routledge.

Murphy, W.D., Haynes, M.R., & Worley, P.J. (1991). Assessment of adult sexual interest. In C.R. Hollin & K. Howells (Eds), *Clinical approaches to sex offenders and their victims.* Chichester: Wiley.

Nabokov, V. (1955). *Lolita.* London: Penguin Books.

Nichols, H.R. & Molinder, I. (1984). *Multiphasic sex inventory manual.* Available from 437 Bowes Drive, Tacoma, WA 98466, USA.

Owen, G. & Steele, N.M. (1991). Incest offenders after treatment. In M.Q. Patton (Ed.), *Family sexual abuse.* London: Sage.

Parker, G., Tupling, H., & Brown, L.B. (1979). A parental bonding instrument. *British Journal of Medical Psychology, 52*, 1–10.

Pithers, W.D., Buell, M.M., Kashima, K.J., Cumming, G.F., & Beal, L.S. (1987). Precursor to sexual offences. *Proceedings of the First Annual Meeting of the Association for the Behavioural Treatment of Sexual Aggressors.* Newport, OR.

Prentky, R.A., Knight, R.A., & Rosenberg, R. (1988). Validation analyses on the MTC taxonomy for rapists: disconfirmation and reconceptualization. In R.A. Prentky & V. Quinsey (Eds), *Human Sexual Aggression: Current Perspectives, 528*, 21–40. New York: The New York Academy of Sciences.

Prochaska, J.O. & DiClemente, C.C. (1982). Transtheoretical psychotherapy: towards a more integrative model of change. *Psychotherapy: Theory, Research and Practice, 19,* 276–278.

Quinsey, V.L., Chaplin, T.C., & Varney, G. (1981). A comparison of rapists and non-sex offenders' sexual preferences for mutually consenting sex, rape and physical abuse of women. *Behavioural Assessment, 3,* 127–135.

Quinsey, V., Harris, G., Rice, M., & Lalumiere, M. (1993). Assessing treatment efficacy in outcome studies of sex offenders. *Journal of Interpersonal Violence, 8,* 512–523.

Quinsey, V.L., Lalumiere, M.L., Rice, M.E., & Harris, G.T. (1995). Predicting sexual offenses. In J. Campbell (Ed.), *Assessing dangerousness—Violence by sexual offenders, batterers and child abusers.* California: Sage.

Rice, M.E., Quinsey, V.L., & Harris, G.T. (1991). Sexual recidivism among child molesters released from a maximum security psychiatric institution. *Journal of Consulting and Clinical Psychology, 59,* 381–386.

Rogers, R. & Dickey, R. (1991). Denial and minimization among sex offenders: A review of competing models of deception. *Annals of Sex Research, 4,* 49–63.

Rosen, I. (1979). *Sexual deviation.* London: Oxford University Press.

Ross, J.E. (1990). *Correctional sex offender treatment program guide-lines.* South Carolina, Jonathan E. Ross, M.A.Inc (cited in Morrison et.al., op.cit., p. 52).

Ryan, G., Lane, S., Davis, J., & Isaac, C. (1987). Juvenile sex offenders: Development and correction. *Child Abuse and Neglect, 11,* 385–395.

Salter, A.C. (1988). *Treating child sex offenders and victims—a practical guide.* California: Sage.

Scully, D. (1990). *Understanding sexual violence: A study of convicted rapists.* London: Harper Collins.

Spence, J.T. & Helmreich, R.L. (1972). The attitudes towards women scale: an objective instrument to measure attitudes toward the rights and roles of women in contemporary society. *Psychological Documents, 2,* 153.

Spence, J.T. & Helmreich, R.L. (1978). *Masculinity and feminity: Their psychological dimensions, correlates and antecedents.* Austin: University of Texas Press.

Steiner, J. (1993). *Psychic retreats: Pathological organizations in psychotic, neurotic and borderline patients.* London: Routledge.

Stevenson, H.C., Castillo, E., & Sefarbi, R. (1989). Treatment of denial in adolescent sex offenders and their families. *Journal of Offender Counseling, Services and Rehabilitation, 14,* 37–50.

Stoller, R.J. (1975). *Perversion: The erotic form of hatred.* New York: Random House.

Thornton, D. & Hogue, T. (1993). The large-scale provision of programmes for imprisoned sex offenders: issues, dilemmas and progress. *Criminal Behaviour and Mental Health, 3,* 371–380.

Thornton, D. & Travers, R. (1991). A longitudinal study of the criminal behaviour of convicted sexual offenders. *Proceedings of the Prison Psychologists' Conference.* HM Prison Service. London: HMSO.

Watson, D. & Friend, R. (1969). Measurement of social-evaluative anxiety. *Journal of Consulting and Clinical Psychology, 33,* 448–457.

Welldon, E. (1996). Let the treatment fit the crime. *Foulkes Lecture.* London, 1996. Unpublished.

Wolf, S.C. (1985). A multifactor model of deviant sexuality. *Victimology: An International Journal, 10,* 359–374.

Author index

Subject index